Advice for Working Dads

HBR WORKING PARENTS SERIES

Tips, stories, and strategies for the job that never ends.

The **HBR Working Parents Series** supports readers as they anticipate challenges, learn how to advocate for themselves more effectively, juggle their impossible schedules, and find fulfillment at home and at work.

From classic issues such as work-life balance and making time for yourself to thorny challenges such as managing an urgent family crisis and the impact of parenting on your career, this series features the practical tips, strategies, and research you need to be—and feel—more effective at home and at work. Whether you're up with a newborn or touring universities with your teen, we've got what you need to make working parenthood work for you.

Books in the series include:

Advice for Working Dads

Advice for Working Moms

Communicate Better with Everyone

Doing It All as a Solo Parent

Getting It All Done

Managing Your Career

Succeeding as a First-Time Parent

Taking Care of Yourself

Two-Career Families

WORKING PARENTS

*Tips, stories, and
strategies for the job
that never ends.*

Advice for
Working Dads

**Harvard Business
Review Press
Boston, Massachusetts**

Copyright 2021 Harvard Business School Publishing Corporation
All rights reserved
Printed in the United States of America

10 9 8 7 6 5 4 3 2 1

No part of this publication may be reproduced, stored in or introduced into a retrieval system, or transmitted, in any form, or by any means (electronic, mechanical, photocopying, recording, or otherwise), without the prior permission of the publisher. Requests for permission should be directed to permissions@harvardbusiness.org, or mailed to Permissions, Harvard Business School Publishing, 60 Harvard Way, Boston, Massachusetts 02163.

The web addresses referenced in this book were live and correct at the time of the book's publication but may be subject to change.

Library of Congress Cataloging-in-Publication Data

Names: Harvard Business Review Press, issuing body.
Title: Advice for working dads.
Other titles: HBR working parents series.
Description: Boston, Massachusetts : Harvard Business Review
    Press, [2021] | Series: Working parents | Includes index.
Identifiers: LCCN 2020054278 (print) | LCCN (ebook) | ISBN
    9781647821012 (paperback) | ISBN 9781647821029 (ebook)
Subjects: LCSH: Fatherhood. | Fathers--Employment. | Parenting. |
    Work-life balance. | Sex discrimination in employment. |
    Sex discrimination against men.
Classification: LCC HQ756 .A363 2021 (print) | LCC HQ756 (ebook) |
    DDC 306.874/2--dc23
LC record available at https://lccn.loc.gov/2020054278
LC ebook record available at https://lccn.loc.gov/2020455395

ISBN: 978-1-64782-101-2
eISBN: 978-1-64782-102-9

The paper used in this publication meets the requirements of the American National Standard for Permanence of Paper for Publications and Documents in Libraries and Archives Z39.48-1992

CONTENTS

Contents

Section 2

Planes to Catch and Bills to Pay

Navigating Fatherhood and Your Career

Contents

Section 3

All Work and No Play . . .
Dedicating Time to Your Family and Yourself

Contents

INTRODUCTION

Starting a New Conversation

by Daisy Dowling

We're about to change the rules of the working-dad game. To get started—and given that you picked up this book in the first place—I'm going to make a few guesses about who you are and what you're grappling with.

First, you're a smart, hardworking man who wants to get ahead. You spend a good percentage of your waking time either actually working or thinking about how to do well on the job. And you're ambitious: With all the sweat equity you're putting into your career, you want it to amount to something.

Second, you love your child—or children, or future children—completely and want nothing but the best for them. That means staying connected and close to them and remaining a central figure, or *the* central figure, in their lives as they grow up. You don't want to only provide for your kids, but *be there* for them, in every sense of the term.

Third, and on top of all your ambition and your incredible commitment to the kids, you *also* want to travel, exercise, see old buddies, volunteer, watch good movies, spend time on your hobbies, or some combination: In other words, you want to be yourself and not fall into the all-too-common but unpleasant trap of being 100% defined by your job, caretaking, and task list.

Fourth, and finally, I'll also guess you don't have many, if *any*, people to model yourself after or talk with in an all-cards-on-the-table kind of way when it comes to how to be a successful, satisfied working dad—in other words, to doing all three of the above at the same time.

Sure, there are other guys out there, and even ones you know or work closely with, who are trying to pull off the same career-kids-self hat trick that you are, but maybe there's not much discussion about fathers as parents at your workplace, and you worry that raising the topic could make you look unambitious or wimpy or even unprofessional. Maybe you admire the senior leaders in your organization and want to hold roles like theirs one day, but it's hard to see yourself in them as a dad who wants to be involved in his kids' daily lives. (It's almost as if some of them live in an alternate, kid-free universe; have they *ever* had to check math homework or change a diaper?) Maybe your own father keeps encouraging you to follow his lead and focus more on your career instead of on the home front. On the other side of the coin, maybe you know some super-dads—the ones who volunteer-coach their kids' sports teams, read Harry Potter aloud, and cook full breakfasts on weekday mornings—but feel that unless you can have yourself cloned, there's no way to do all that *and* accomplish what you need to at work. Perhaps you've looked into joining your organization's working-parents network, but found it was mostly moms and/or mostly parents of younger kids; you've looked for working-parent peers only to find you don't fit in. Maybe it's impossible to find the time to do the stuff that makes you *you*, and when you do, you end up giving yourself flak for it or worry your partner will. And in the absence of role models, mentors, peers, and constructive conversation—without working-dad validation, connections, or a crew—you find yourself trying to soldier through the career-plus-children challenge quietly, and on your own.

But here's the thing: It's *not* just you. As an executive coach who specializes in advising working parents in high-pressure roles and intense environments, I spend my days talking one-on-one with men and women trying to hammer together their demanding careers and devotion to family. They *all* have logistical, personal, and career concerns, although the moms much more often report having circles of "working-mom friends" they can turn to, senior women they can pattern themselves on, and mentors they can speak to frankly about work-life matters. Finding the right support may not be *easy* for women, but openness about work-plus-caregiving concerns is more common, allowable, expected. A mom planning her parental leave can find herself inundated with advice from colleagues, but as a dad you may worry about the career signal you're sending in taking any leave at all. When you saw this book's title, it may even have struck you as strange because c'mon, who even talks about "working dads"?

Well, we will—right here, in this book. That hide-and-deny, go-it-alone thing: it ends now. In the pages ahead, we'll start a whole new conversation: an honest one about how you can succeed at work, be an awesome father, and stay yourself, too. And if we're *ever* going to start that conversation, this is the right time. If the Covid-19 pandemic did nothing else useful for us, it encouraged (or forced) us, and our organizations, to acknowledge and be more open about our working-parent realities, and helped prompt us toward new ways of thinking and new approaches, as parents, professionals, people.

Advice for Working Dads puts your most pressing and prominent concerns right out there in center field and gives you new ways to see them and act on them. The experts you'll hear from throughout this collection know exactly what you're dealing with, they come with zero attitude about it, and they're ready with actionable, practical, and road-tested solutions for you to try. Whether you're dealing with a boss who just assumes that your partner will handle all of the parenting logistics, or are parenting three school-age kids while pushing for a promotion, or are tackling any other common working-dad concerns, the chapters in *Advice for Working Dads* will help. If you've had enough of being walled off from other working dads and enough pretending that you're not committed to your career *and* your kids—or feeling too often as if you have to choose one or the other or put both ahead of yourself—then this book is the right one for you.

You're short on time and want to use this book practically and efficiently, so begin by thinking to yourself, "What are the two or three pieces of working fatherhood that cause the most stress and strain for me?" If you could sit down, confidentially, with a few really smart mentors and have them coach you on some aspect of working fatherhood, what would you ask them? Then flip to the contents. You'll see a good place to begin reading, whether that's Han-Son Lee's chapter on how to find allies and advisers at work, Mark McCartney's piece on reclaiming family time, Stewart Friedman's chapter on how your work affects your children, or any one of the other two dozen practical chapters you'll find here.

As you read, remember that you're participating in a whole new conversation. You'll hear fresh, authoritative voices and ideas, and you'll be pushed to try out new habits and tactics. Because of that candor and because you're being nudged a little, you may even feel mildly uncomfortable, and not every suggestion you find here will apply to or work for you. That's OK, because this is your family and career. You make the decisions, and you'll know what's right.

After trying some of the tips and strategies, you'll find something else happening, too: That old awkwardness or hesitation on working-dad matters will start to fall away. The phrase "working dad" won't seem strange or new anymore. You'll just be a smart, hardworking, ambitious guy who wants to get ahead, who loves his children completely, and who has a strong, confident sense of how to do both authentically *and* be the person you want to be and connect with others who want to do same.

Section 1

We Can Do It, Too!

Burying Old Working-Dad Clichés

The Three Types of Working Father

by Brad Harrington

Quick Takes

- Identify the type of working father you are: traditional, egalitarian, or conflicted

- Understand how your type affects your caregiving habits and aspirations

- Make adjustments to raise your level of satisfaction at home and work

I t has been widely discussed that dads today want to be much more involved in their children's day-to-day lives than fathers were a generation ago. Yet this shift from the "Traditional Dad" or "Boomer Dad" toward the "New Dad" or "Millennial Dad" remains little examined. How many working dads are walking this untraditional path? Are they truly embracing a 50/50 split in caregiving? And how can a better understanding of these trends help individual fathers find success in the workplace and at home?

My organization, the Boston College Center for Work & Family, has endeavored to answer these questions. A decade ago, fathers were conspicuously absent when it came to work and family research and corporate policies. Employers, the field of research, and society as a whole seemed content to continue to paint dads simply as breadwinners. To address this gap, we began the New Dad research series of annual reports, exploring the experiences of today's fathers and how their roles are changing—and how they're not.[1]

Painting an accurate description of today's working dads is a herculean task, so we narrowed our focus to professional, college-educated fathers who mainly worked in large corporations. Our research has looked at a range of fathers and from a number of different perspectives—new fathers, fathers in dual-career couples, dads of different generations (baby boomers, Gen Xers, and millennials), even at-home dads. We explored their attitudes about their employers, their managers and colleagues, career success, parental leave, shared caregiving, and life and work fulfillment. One of the most important insights this work has yielded is that the "Millennial Dad" paradigm isn't simply replacing "Boomer Dad" paradigms in the workplace. Instead, today's working fathers are split between three groups with different desires, concerns, and areas of challenge.

The Three Types of "New Dad"

Most dads no longer see their role solely or even primarily as a breadwinner. In our research, between 70% and 75% want to share parenting responsibilities equally with their partner. They also *need* to do more on the home front as women take on roles of greater responsibility in the workplace and, increasingly, are higher earners than their partners.

But there is also a noticeable drop-off between fathers' good intentions on shared parenting and reality. So, in

2016, we began to look more deeply at what fathers were struggling with when trying to rectify the distance between their aspirations and their actions.

Our research uncovered many conflicts that dads face. For example, they regularly state they want to spend more time with their children, but they also want to take on a work role with greater responsibility. Inconsistencies like that show up often. Two questions made this most clear to us:

- How do you *think* caregiving should be divided between you and your spouse/partner?

- How *is* caregiving divided between you and your spouse/partner?

From an analysis of the responses, we discovered that fathers fell into one of three groups. The first we called *traditional fathers*. These men stated that their wives should do more on the caregiving front, and she did do more. The second group, which we called *egalitarian fathers*, said that caregiving should be divided 50/50 and felt that it was the case. The third group felt they should be sharing caregiving 50/50 but admitted their wives were doing more than they were. We labeled them *conflicted fathers*. Interestingly, each group constituted roughly one-third of our sample, although in our more recent studies, the percentage of egalitarian fathers has increased slightly. (Sadly but unsurprisingly, fathers who did a true majority of caregiving were not statistically significant in our study.)

Looking at these three groups of fathers separately revealed three very different experiences of working fatherhood.

- Egalitarian fathers reported the highest levels of satisfaction across the vast majority of wide-ranging questions about their work and home lives. Even when it came to finding it easy to balance work and family, the egalitarians' scores were the most positive in spite of the fact that they were doing the most on the home front.

- Traditional fathers scored somewhat lower, except in two areas: satisfaction with earnings and career advancement.

- Conflicted fathers scored lower on virtually every satisfaction and fulfillment indicator, from feeling respected in their work group to finding it easy to balance work and family. They experienced the most challenges at home and at work. The biggest falloff was a statement to measure overall life satisfaction, "I would change almost nothing about my life." 82% of egalitarian fathers agreed; for conflicted fathers, the number plummeted to 33%.

No one would imply that egalitarian working dads "have it all" or that traditional working dads have the luxury of focusing solely on their careers. But the fact is that conflicted dads are truly struggling, often due to circumstances beyond their control.

The Conflicted-Dad Dilemma

Why is it the case that this dissonance occurs so often, in nearly one out of three dads? Many conversations, interviews, and studies I have engaged in over the past decade make me believe the following factors lead to these conflicted feelings:

- Fathers continue to be defined primarily as breadwinners rather than caretakers. This image of fathers has existed for a long time, and it clearly won't change overnight. Most men were raised to believe this was their primary role in and contribution to the family, and this depiction of men is often reinforced by friends and relatives, employers, the media, and society at large.

- In spite of the growing number of households where women are the primary breadwinners, the reality is that even in dual-career couples, fathers' financial contributions to the family are greater than their partner's in three out of four households, so their salary is needed more.[2] This financial imbalance weighs into nearly every conversation I have about why men don't share caregiving equally. (The economic argument wins out in both directions: The relatively rare fathers who become at-home dads nearly always have lower earning potential than their partners.)

- Organizations have been slow to catch up to and accept men's expanded role in the home. It is still the case that the most senior leaders in organizations are men, and many have stay-at-home spouses. As a result, senior managers lack understanding of their millennial father employees' lives. Thankfully, this is beginning to change, as there is a growing recognition that most couples these days are dual-career, so dads need to be major players on the caregiving front as well.

- Historically, men have not been offered paid paternity leave. This lack of time flying solo caring for newborns leads to lower levels of confidence and competence in caregiving for men. And once mothers have spent months at home being the primary caregiver, the gendered parenting roles have been firmly established.

What Conflicted Dads Can Do

As stated, we have consistently found that most dads aspire to be more equal caregivers, but clearly the actions of many fathers need to change to meet their aspirations. Our institutions and society need to support men in their caregiving role. But individuals also have an important role to play in catalyzing this movement forward. Here are a few suggestions for fathers:

- Talk to other fathers formally or informally to share common struggles and brainstorm potential solutions. If a fathers' employee resource group (ERG) does not exist in your organization, consider establishing one with your fellow dads in conjunction with your employer's human resource department. Father groups are also growing in many local communities providing social connections and support, especially for at-home dads.

- Invite speakers into your organization for brown-bag sessions dedicated to fathers. This can be on the changing role of fathers, parenting skills, or achieving greater fit between work and family life. I am often asked to speak at corporations on the topic of today's fathers and frequently get this feedback from attendees: "This is the first time there has been a conversation in the organization about working dads."

- If your organization offers paternity leave, strongly consider taking this time off to bond with your child and to gain experience in hands-on parenting. Our research indicates there are a number of benefits to doing so. It will increase your confidence and competence in your parenting skills (92% of fathers who took leave agreed). It will also help you establish early on your role as a co-caregiver and strengthen your relationship with your partner (83% of fathers agreed), your bond with your child (96% of fathers agreed), and your sense of life satisfaction (88% of fathers agreed).

- Have frequent conversations with your spouse or partner about your respective roles at home and your goals for your family. Our research has demonstrated that couples who hold these discussions more frequently are likely to have higher marital and life satisfaction.

- Support other fathers in your workplace who are caregivers. Changing organizational culture requires more than changes in policies or statements of support from senior leaders. Men who support colleagues in their effort to be engaged parents will help to shift the organizational culture to one that is more equitable and encouraging of men as caregivers. This will, in turn, also help to promote the advancement of women in the organization.

What Organizations Can Do

Organizational policies and culture that are unfriendly to working dads (or ignore them altogether) bear much responsibility for the prevalence of conflicted fathers. Organizations would benefit from realizing that dissatisfied employees are disengaged employees and that fathers who don't feel supported by their employers will be increasingly hard to retain.

- Offer paternity leave. Since our 2014 study of paternity leave, we have seen the beginnings of a dramatic shift in fathers being offered and taking paid leave. More and more large employers are offering expanded paid parental leave on a gender-neutral basis, often as much as 6–20 weeks of fully paid time off. And, contrary to the conventional wisdom that men won't take leave if offered, fathers *are* taking advantage of this new offering, and those who do are the greatest advocates for their fellow fathers to do the same.

- Improve cultural acceptance of fathers as care-givers. As a starting point, survey fathers in your organization to assess whether they feel the climate is as accepting of fathers' engagement as caregivers as it is for mothers. Ask them for recommendations on what the organization can do to improve this aspect of the corporate culture.

- Consider offering development opportunities for men to reflect on and address their work-life challenges. This could include programs such as an in-depth career management course that allows participants to examine their values, look for disconnects between those values and their actions, and develop a career-life plan. Helping fathers better understand and take steps to resolve their feelings of conflict should result in happier and more engaged employees.

Looking Forward

Fathers are increasingly realizing the importance of balance between their work and family responsibilities, but many still struggle with this balancing act. We hope that our findings encourage them to rededicate themselves to the mission of equalizing caregiving with their partners.

Today, the outlook is mixed. On the positive side, the number of egalitarian fathers in our surveys has crept up, slowly but steadily, since 2015. But the profound impact of the coronavirus pandemic on working parents seems to have beckoned the return of some outdated gender stereotypes about who should be doing what. As a result, many more mothers than fathers have been forced to scale back their work roles or leave the labor force altogether. Fathers and organizations must accelerate their efforts to make a 50/50 split a reality. In the long run, the fathers, their partners, and their children will benefit greatly from their determination to do so.

2

What's a Working Dad to Do?

by Scott Behson

Quick Takes

- Own your role in changing the conversation about working fathers
- Talk about your family at work and ask other men about theirs
- Start an informal group to discuss your lives outside of work
- Use work flexibility—and ensure that others see you doing it
- Take your full paternity leave to model behavior to others

was once on a radio show to discuss the struggles men face in trying to balance work and family demands. During the interview, the cohost told a quick anecdote about a run-in he had when he was a rising corporate lawyer at a prestigious New York City firm. He was divorced and his ex-wife and his kids lived in London, so he flew there to see his kids every other weekend. After two monster weeks of work, he was heading out of the office to go to JFK Airport late one Thursday afternoon when a more senior partner confronted him, saying, "Where are you going?"

The cohost responded, explaining that he'd bulked up the past two weeks to finish his work for his very satisfied client and that he was catching his flight to Heathrow to see his kids. The partner angrily responded, "Bullshit. You see your kids more than I do, and I live with mine. Besides I need you here tonight—and over the weekend." The cohost pushed back and caught his flight, but shortly thereafter decided to give up his career as a lawyer. Life was just too short.

This is an extreme example, but many working fathers face similar pressures to conform to a traditional gender role that insists they be "all in" for work, regardless of achievement level and regardless of family responsibilities. And this is the case despite the facts that:

- Dual-income, shared-care families are far more the norm than families with a single-earner and an at-home spouse.

- Today's fathers spend three times as much time with their children and twice as much time on housework than dads did a generation ago.

- Men aspire to be even more involved in their families than they are.[1]

As a result, it has been reported that dads experience at least as much work-family conflict as mothers, and that in some ways, men are facing a funhouse-mirror version of women's struggles to attain success at both work and home.[2]

A few years ago, the Flexibility Stigma Working Group at the Center for WorkLife Law at the UC Hastings College of the Law, consisting of researchers from over a dozen universities, published a series of research studies in a special issue of the *Journal of Social Issues* entitled "The Flexibility Stigma." About half of the articles focus on barriers men face in the workplace as they try to balance work and family demands. Among their findings:

- While men value work flexibility, they are reluctant to seek out flexible work arrangements because of fears of being seen as uncommitted and unmanly, and expectations of potential career consequences. These fears, unfortunately, prove to be well founded.

- Fathers who engage in higher-than-average levels of childcare are subject to more workplace harassment (for example, picked on for "not being man enough") and more general mistreatment (for example, garden-variety workplace aggression) as compared to their low-caregiving or childless counterparts.

- Men requesting family leave are perceived as uncommitted to work and less masculine; these perceptions are linked to lower performance evaluations, increased risks of being demoted or downsized, and reduced pay and rewards.

- Finally, men who interrupt their employment for family reasons earn significantly less after returning to work.

All in all, that's a pretty stark set of findings. What's a working father to do? The first step toward healthier workplace culture is to bring the fathers' work-family issue out of the shadows and to make it a topic for discussion—and that starts with fathers themselves.

As Gandhi said, "We need to be the change we wish to see." If you have the security, flexibility, courage, and inclination (I recognize some may have more ability to do this at work than others), here are four things working dads can do in our workplaces to make it easier for all of us to discuss and address our work-family concerns.

- While at work, **talk about your family** and ask other men about theirs.

- Reach out to some male work friends and **start an informal group** to discuss your lives outside of work. Have lunch together or grab a drink after work and talk.

- **Use work flexibility** and let your male colleagues see you do so. Tell people you are leaving early for a school event but are taking work home. Or, explain why working from home a few days a week is so valuable, since you're able to replace commuting time with helping your kids with their schoolwork.

- At the birth of a new child, **take your full paternity leave**. Make a plan and communicate it to others in your company, signaling your commitment as a dedicated father and employee. (As a leader or manager, this is especially important, as others will model your behavior.)

We need to make it more normal for working fathers to discuss and address family issues. I know it is not easy to stand out. But these small steps can lay the groundwork for communicating your needs as a parent and building more supportive workplace cultures.

Adapted from content posted on hbr.org, August 21, 2013.

It's Time for Working Dads to Lead by Example

by Tim Allen

Quick Takes

- Stop contributing to a work culture that is unfriendly to working dads
- Working during family time sends a message to other dads that they'll be stigmatized if they don't
- Take *all* of your paternity leave, and truly disconnect from work
- Make your work-life boundaries clear so that your colleagues and employees can do the same

The day my twin sons were born was the happiest of my life. There is one thing I regret though: the conference call I was wrapping up with my executive team as I raced through the hospital doors.

I wish I could take that call back. But in that whirlwind moment, coupled with my happiness was the immense weight of expectation. As a CEO, I felt an external responsibility to be available. No matter what.

My always-on work ethos didn't stop there. Instead of taking all of the paid paternity leave that my company, IAC, generously offered, I took one week . . . stretched out over the course of a few weeks. But even during my time at home—thrown into the elation, novelty, and sleeplessness (did I mention they were twins?) of new parenthood—I kept working. I took phone calls and answered emails. I looked at spreadsheets and made decisions. *Business doesn't stop, so neither can I*, I told myself. *Hundreds of people at work are depending on me. I can't let them down.* I wouldn't allow myself to fully disconnect, not even for one week.

This is a common problem among working dads, especially senior leaders and managers. Even while employers are increasingly offering paid paternity leave benefits (the Society for Human Resource Management's 2019 Employee Benefits Survey found an increase in paternity leave benefits from 21% in 2016 to 30% in 2019), most new dads take significantly less time than their benefit allows.[1] Of the fathers who do take paid leave (if it's offered), 70% return to work in 10 days or less, according to the U.S. Department of Labor.[2] A key reason why? Unsupportive leadership. In a 2019 study by the Boston College Center for Work & Family, 55% of men said they didn't feel extremely supported by senior management in their decision to take paternity leave.[3]

It's impossible to overstate how much paternity leave matters. The longer a father is on leave, the better it is for a child's development, as well as for gender equity both at home and at work. Studies have found that men who take leave, particularly more than two weeks, develop closer bonds with their children and stronger, more equal relationships with their partner, and are less likely to get divorced.

My boys are five now, and my partner and I are more worried about them starting kindergarten than sleepless nights. And it's taken introspection and experience as both a father and a leader to admit a hard truth: By not taking all my paternity leave—and working while I should have been off—I was letting my sons down as their dad and my partner down as a co-parent. And, through my example as a leader, I was letting down the other parents at my company.

Again, the problem wasn't my paternity benefits—my company had the right policies in place. The problem was the disconnect between written policy and actual culture. I was contributing to a norm that company comes first and being a dad comes second. When I took that call on the day of my sons' birth, I was unwittingly sending a message to other dads at my office that they'd be stigmatized if they didn't do the same. I was communicating that they'd be marginalized in their career advancement and perceived as being less committed to their job if they showed commitment as a parent.

Dad-unfriendly work cultures fester in other insidious ways. Male leaders and managers will often hide their parenting responsibilities from their teams or not take advantage of flexible work arrangements available to them so they can project the "ideal worker" image. Other working dads are pressured to follow that behavior. Care .com conducted a survey during the summer of the 2020 Covid-19 pandemic that found that 51% of working dads sometimes hide their childcare concerns because they worry their employer or colleagues won't understand.[4]

These behaviors perpetuate unhealthy and, frankly, unrealistic expectations for working dads—and breed a culture that's shrouded in lies and built on burnout.

What happens when company culture supports working dads?

A dad-friendly culture has a halo effect that benefits working mothers, too—and the positive effects reverberate throughout the organization.

Furthering gender equality. Historically, the false assumption has been that men don't need to worry about childcare—that's what moms are for. So, when men enter senior leadership positions, they often fail to make caregiving a priority inside their organization because balancing parenting and work hasn't been an issue for *their* careers.

It's certainly been a huge issue for women's careers, though. Numerous studies have confirmed this, including the *2020 Women in the Workplace* report by LeanIn .org and McKinsey & Company, which surveyed more than 300 companies and more than 40,000 employees from the entry level to the C-suite.[5] Not only are mothers doing more work at home than fathers, but they are also more than twice as likely as fathers to worry that they're being judged more harshly at work because of their caregiving obligations at home. They're also far less comfortable than fathers at sharing their work-life challenges with colleagues or even the fact that they are parents at all.

The Covid-19 pandemic amplified this reality and made things worse. With childcare centers closed and schools going virtual or hybrid, women have taken on even more childcare work at home. And they're dropping out of the workforce as a result, particularly those in senior leadership and Black women. This is erasing decades of progress toward gender equality. As of September 2020, the percentage of women participating in the U.S. workforce dropped to 55.6%, down from a peak of 60.3% in April 2000.[6]

The only way to achieve gender equality at work is to embolden male employees and give them the support they need at work so they can be more involved at home, while allowing their partners to work, too.

Attracting and retaining talented working parents. Business leaders who don't support working fathers risk losing them to companies that do. Nearly 70% of working dads say they would change jobs to spend more time with their kids, according to a 2018 study by Promundo and Dove Men + Care.[7]

Retaining talented parents starts by understanding, talking, and listening to them. Get their feedback through surveys to uncover their struggles. Use employee resource groups to have open, honest communication. Consider joining one yourself and participate on equal footing.

Working parents also need to feel encouraged to face their fears and have honest conversations with management, however uncomfortable, about what they need. In these conversations, you may discover that one-size-fits-all parental benefits aren't always helpful and that parents need more tailored options.

Research has shown that successful leaders adopt a growth and learning mindset, both for themselves and for the business. Adopt this same thinking about your working-parent workforce. Care about them as much as you do your next product launch or your quarterly earnings.

Committing to the culture

Before I accepted my role as CEO of Care.com, I committed to a new work-life philosophy: I was a dad first, and to be a great leader, I needed to bring my authentic self to work. I made it clear to my new leadership team and employees that I expected them to adopt the same philosophy. The mission of Care.com is to help families balance their lives and work while caring for all they love. We couldn't as a company deliver on that mission if we didn't embody it ourselves.

As CEO, it started with me, but it takes leaders and managers throughout any organization to set the right example for our employees. We must be cognizant of the attitudes and behaviors that compound to create a stressful culture for working parents. During my week of leave, I'd often get asked by colleagues to have a quick call . . . "just five minutes." I felt the obligation to say yes—and, of course, that call turned into several "quick" five-minute calls. If leaders and managers don't draw boundaries, then nobody else in the company will either.

So, as a leader, be vulnerable, honest, and empathetic about your life as a parent. Encourage other dads in the company to do the same. Ensure that all the parents at your organization have access to great benefits like paid leave, backup care, and flexible work schedules. And, make sure you use them so that they do, too.

A few weeks ago, I was on a Zoom call with my team and was surprised to see a senior manager who I knew was supposed to be on his family vacation. Instinctively, I told him, "I really appreciate your commitment, but you're not supposed to be working right now. I'll catch up with you when you're back from spending time with your family." With his kids visible in the background, he got the message and quickly hung up.

I wasn't just talking to him; I was talking to everyone on that call, including myself.

Adapted from "I'm a CEO and a Working Dad. Here's What I Wish I Did Differently," on hbr.org, December 8, 2020 (product #H06151).

End the "Nice Guy" Backlash

by David M. Mayer

Quick Takes

Men are penalized when they stray from masculine stereotypes. To combat this, we should:

- Celebrate men who engage in positive behaviors

- Train employees more broadly about gender stereotypes

- Stop "gender policing"

When women behave in ways that don't fit their gender stereotype—for example, by being assertive—they are viewed as less likable and ultimately less hirable.[1] Does the same hold true for men? Are they similarly penalized for straying from the strong masculine stereotype?

The short answer is yes. Research demonstrates that men too face backlash when they don't adhere to masculine gender stereotypes—when they show vulnerability, act nicer, display empathy, express sadness, exhibit modesty, and proclaim to be feminists. This is troubling not least because it discourages men from behaving in ways known to benefit their teams and their own careers. Let's look at each of these behaviors.

Showing vulnerability

Men are socialized to not ask for help or be vulnerable, and they can be penalized when they challenge this notion. An informative set of studies from 2015 finds that when male (but not female) leaders ask for help, they are viewed as less competent, capable, and confident.[2] And when men make themselves vulnerable by disclosing a weakness at work, they are perceived to have lower status.[3] This is problematic, as not seeking help when you need it or admitting areas for improvement inevitably leads to mistakes and less development.

Being nicer

Given that many of us want more nice guys at work, we might assume that men would be celebrated for being calm and unassuming. Wrong. Research has found that men who are more communal and agreeable (for example, warm, caring, supportive, sympathetic) made significantly less money than more stereotypically masculine men. More agreeable men across multiple industries made an average of 18% less in income and were evaluated as less likely to have management potential as compared to less agreeable men.[4]

Similarly, "nice guys" were evaluated as less competent and less hirable for managerial roles.[5] One experimental study found that male managers in consulting who tended to advocate more for their team than for themselves were judged to be lower in agency and competence and more likely to be considered for job dismissal.[6] Unfortunately, given the costs—real and psychological—of being a nice guy at work, men may be less likely to engage in these behaviors that could help their own career and make them better colleagues.

Displaying empathy

Empathy is an important part of leadership. However, women are more likely to receive credit for it than men. A recent study found that female leaders who displayed empathy (as reported by their employees) were less likely to be in danger of career derailment—for example, problems with interpersonal relationships, difficulty building and leading teams, difficulty changing and adapting, failure in meeting business goals and objectives, and having too narrow a functional orientation.[7] Men did not get this boost—there was no relationship between male leaders' empathy and their bosses' assessment of potential career derailment. These findings are consequential because displaying empathy is critical for leading effectively.

Expressing sadness

U.S. men are socialized to be stoic. What happens when they show emotions other than anger? Research demonstrates that men who show sadness at work are thought of as less deserving of that emotion compared to sad women.[8] A study from 2017 found that men who cry at work are perceived as more emotional and less competent than women who cry.[9] And when men cry in response to performance feedback, the feedback provider rates them as a lower performer, less likely to get promoted, and less capable, compared to women who cry.[10] While we don't want men or women regularly crying at work, an authentic work environment has to allow all employees to experience the same emotions without penalty.

Exhibiting modesty

What happens when men display modesty? Research demonstrates that men who were more humble in expressing their qualifications were evaluated as less likable, less agentic, and weaker than modest women.[11] Similarly, men in the hiring process who were more self-effacing were evaluated by potential employers as lower in competence and less desirable to hire, compared to self-effacing women.[12] With the increasing awareness of the detrimental effects of narcissism at work, we should encourage men's modesty rather than penalize it.[13]

Being a feminist or feminine

As noted previously, a sizable percentage of American men self-identify as being a feminist. However, research indicates that feminist men are more likely to be the victims of sexual harassment—from being told inappropriate jokes to being the recipient of unwanted sexual advances.[14] In addition, research shows that men are more likely to be harassed when they work in male-dominated jobs and are perceived as too feminine.[15] Research finds that men who ask for family leave, something that was historically in the purview of women, are viewed as poorer workers and are less recommended for rewards, compared to female counterparts.[16] We should be welcoming feminist men, rather than derogating them for not being "man enough."

Can we stop penalizing good behavior from men?

Organizations have a stake in ensuring that men aren't penalized for these behaviors—which not only help men's own and their team's performance, but also create a culture that supports gender equality. So what can we do?

Celebrate men who engage in positive behaviors

It is important for men who display these nice-guy qualities to be well received by organizational leadership. For example, when negotiating pay, organizations should not give in to a man who is dominant, but instead try to make sure men are paid based on merit. In addition, given the many benefits of humility, organizations should create a culture where men who are humble are praised. Organizational leaders can champion men in the organization by telling stories about how their vulnerability helped the organization perform better.

Train more broadly about gender stereotypes

Diversity training often evokes skepticism from employees—especially men. One way to address this issue is to focus on how gender stereotypes about women *and* men impact expectations for how they should behave. Given that white men are more likely to feel defensive when organizations provide diversity training, highlighting how men and women are both victims of gender stereotypes can help invoke compassion from all trainees.[17]

Do not "gender police"

Gender policing means imposing normative gender expressions in terms of behavior or appearance. Research shows that trying to make men adhere to gender norms, for example, in terms of attire, is detrimental in terms of allowing men to fully express themselves at work.[18] Workplaces that allow for authentic expression in terms of dress and demeanor will be more attractive to employees, especially millennials.

It is an important time to encourage a more modern form of masculinity. Organizations can and should celebrate traditional aspects of masculinity such as responsibility, assertiveness, and competitiveness, as well as compassion, humility, and kindness. This is not only the right thing to do but also will create the type of environment in which men, women, and organizations will thrive.

Adapted from "How Men Get Penalized for Straying from Masculine Norms" on hbr.org, October 8, 2018 (product #H04JYI).

Dads, Commit to Your Family at Home and at Work

by Haley Swenson, Eve Rodsky, David G. Smith, and W. Brad Johnson

Quick Takes

- Acknowledge the gap in unpaid work at home
- Aim for equity in household tasks
- Collaborate with your partner on decision making
- Speak up at work about your family's needs

Fathers are increasingly recognizing the value of participating in the everyday work of caring for, educating, and raising their children. But changing long-standing social dynamics doesn't happen overnight or without conscious effort. It is critical that men engage as fully as possible in sharing the work at home. This should start with an honest assessment of where progress is happening, and where it has stalled.

Where Dads Are—and Aren't—Contributing

A pre-pandemic study from the Better Life Lab at New America found that fathers were already valuing their familial role as they never had before.[1] The study, which included a nationally representative survey of men and women from across the United States and five on-line focus groups, set out to determine what aspects of fathering participants deem "very important," and the answers are surprising. Though the notion of dads as financial providers has traditionally prevailed as their main contribution to their kids, this priority fell toward the bottom of the list. At the top were "showing love and affection" and "teaching the child about life." And the vast majority of fathers reported engaging in a variety of parenting tasks on a daily basis, from cooking meals and handling certain household chores to providing transportation and soothing and nurturing them. Other research has shown that since the 1970s, fathers have tripled the amount of time they spend in the unpaid work of tending to their kids and home.[2]

While this is certainly progress, fathers, on average, still do only around *half* of the unpaid work that mothers do (see figure 5-1). While parents of both genders in the Better Life Lab study said they *played* with their kids on a daily basis at about the same rates, moms were more likely to take on all the other tasks every day.

Without dads doing a more equitable share of this work—especially during the pandemic—moms will continue to struggle with that "double shift" of paid and unpaid labor, which both maintains gender inequities and creates psychological distress and burnout.[3]

So where do fathers need to step up? The biggest gaps between what moms and dads say they do for their kids is in helping with education and managing schedules and other activities. This finding reflects something researchers have long noted: Some parenting tasks are less visible and come with a higher "mental load" than others—and mothers are more likely to be responsible for them.[4] One recent study found that women reported

FIGURE 5-1

Mothers are more likely to take on daily tasks compared to fathers

Without dads doing a more equitable share of this work—especially during the pandemic—moms will continue to struggle with that "double shift" of paid and unpaid labor, which both maintains gender inequities and creates psychological distress and burnout.

Percent who say they do these
childcare activities on a daily basis:

■ FATHERS   ▨ MOTHERS

Make meals or feed children
76%
94%

Comfort, soothe, and provide emotional support
73%
89%

Provide transportation
70%
83%

Play with children
65%
70%

Handle household chores
59%
75%

Manage schedules or activities
54%
74%

Discipline children
52%
67%

Take part in educational activities
51%
71%

Source: Better Life Lab at New America, 2020

doing more "cognitive labor" for the family—such as anticipating needs (*The kids are due for annual physicals*), monitoring progress (*Are they up to date on all of their boosters?*), identifying options (*What day are they free for appointments?*), and making decisions (*We'll make the appointment for the Friday after next*).[5] This work is time consuming and often exhausting. Worse, fathers report little awareness of it, which can have deleterious effects on marital relationships and mothers' paid work.

Solutions for Families

What will it take to get more men involved in household work, both visible and invisible? First, men need to recognize what they're *not* doing and add it to their to-do lists. Here are some actions that fathers can take to help themselves and their families.

Acknowledge the aspiration-execution gap

While most fathers believe they're sharing equitably in unpaid work at home, evidence clearly shows that they're not.[6] Initiate an honest conversation with your partner about who does what, and how much time things take. According to research in *Fair Play*, a book written by one of our coauthors, Eve Rodsky, the biggest hurdle to these types of conversations is being hesitant to initiate an invitation to sit down with your partner for fear of being "rejected," "dismissed," or "misunderstood." Using a gamified invitation tool can bring levity and remove emotion from the conversation.[7]

Aim for equity, rather than a 50/50 split

Eve also argues that the focus should be on each partner "owning" a set of domestic responsibilities—from conception to planning through execution. Discuss and agree in advance on the value of each task. Then decide who should do what based on availability, capability, and an understanding that doing the time-intensive housework and childcare traditionally shouldered by women shouldn't be a life sentence for one person or determined by a gender role.[8] This will result in a fair rather than even split. Studies have shown that perceived fairness by both parties is a stronger predictor of a healthy marriage than the actual division of domestic labor.

What does this look like, in practical terms? Approaching these conversations with your partner using an ownership mindset is key to fairness. If it's your job to handle your kids' extracurricular sports, it's not just showing up every Saturday to the Little League field. It's also submitting medical forms, picking up uniforms, ordering cleats (and then returning them when they don't fit), remembering to pack the kids' sunscreen and water bottles, and arranging carpools for practice.

Collaborate with your partner in advance on short-term and long-term decision making

Making intentional choices and customizing your defaults about who does what decreases daily decision fatigue and allows you to make intentional choices together. Specifically, couples can use contracts to set expectations in advance. There is life-changing magic in this kind of short- and long-term thinking. Life becomes a lot easier if you know who is setting the dinner table before anyone is hangry.

Support your partner's career unconditionally

Research shows that in the long term, successful dual-career couples trade off in prioritizing one partner's career over the other's throughout their working lives together.[9] In particular, male partners in hetero cisgender relationships, who may be used to more traditional gender roles and scripts, can initiate conversations about how to plan for these moments to show support for their partners' career demands and responsibilities. If you find career demands are higher for your spouse, adjust your own career and support them unconditionally.

Speak up at work

Sticking to your long-term vision for equity in your partnership may require difficult conversations at work. Despite the stigma associated with men taking advantage of parental leave, family sick leave, and flexible work arrangements, now is the time for men to initiate conversations with managers and bosses about access to these benefits.[10]

If you don't know if you're ready to advocate for yourself, build a coalition of fathers within your organization to create consensus and speak with a collective voice. Talk to your work colleagues. Josh Levs, author of *All In*, suggests that it's very helpful when men just strike up a conversation with women or other men in the workplace and say something like, "Hey, I'm having trouble figuring out how to get my kid to school before work. How do you do it?" And when you decide to approach your boss, know your company's policies, have a plan, and be realistic in setting boundaries and expectations.

• • •

These issues mark only a few of the incredible challenges families confront, and women should not bear the weight of them alone. Fathers say they're ready to engage more at home, and the time for action is now: Gender equality can't wait.

Adapted from content posted on hbr.org, November 11, 2020 (product #BG2005).

Planes to Catch and Bills to Pay

*Navigating Fatherhood
and Your Career*

Breaking Out of the "Working Dad's Career Trap"

by Scott Behson

Quick Takes

If you find yourself in a career that no longer fits your life priorities:

- Get over the idea that stepping back is a failure

- Explore flexible and remote work

- Look for father-friendly employers

- Consider different industry sectors

- Recognize and adjust to financial trade-offs

Today's working fathers care about success both in their careers and at home. They take pride in being good providers for their families and dedicating the time and effort necessary to be loving fathers, partners, and spouses.[1] But many find that their career success cuts both ways. Some find themselves enmeshed in a career that, while it has many merits, may no longer fit their full range of life priorities, especially as fathers, and keeps them from feeling fully successful at work and home. As one dad I worked with told me:

> *I always swore I'd get off the road after my son was in school and in travel basketball, but it is hard to turn down work when the family depends on me—plus I love my job. But now, I fear I'm really missing out. I always wanted to coach basketball, but I make, at best, one-third of the games as it is. I know my wife has sacrificed more of her career than we initially bargained for, and this is putting a strain on our relationship. When I'm around, I'm a loving dad,*

*but I think my son feels my absence. I know things
are off but can't quite figure out how to make a
change.*

Feelings like this can be brought on by having a first
baby or milestone birthdays, or realizing how much
their lives have changed in the years since they made
foundational career choices. I call it the "working dad's
career trap."

Once you commit to excelling in a demanding career,
it becomes hard to scale back without jeopardizing all
that you've worked and sacrificed for. Partner tracks
and corporate ladders are not known for accommodat-
ing those who try to revise the deal. Our earning power,
health insurance, and retirement plans can be weighty
golden handcuffs. Big-time income also often means financial commitments to such expenditures as private
schools or jumbo mortgages.

This dilemma is especially troublesome because most
working fathers are just entering the *harvesting phase*, in
James Citrin's model of career progression—the stage in
which one's years of hard work begin to translate into
positions of significantly higher salary, reputation, influence, and marketability. Being in the harvesting stage
incents you to keep on your current path.[2]

I conduct a prioritization exercise with working dads
who feel torn between the path they are on and where

they want to be in their lives. I ask them to allocate points to three categories of career priorities:

A. Security, income, advancement

B. Interesting work, accomplishment, helping others

C. Flexible work with independence and time for life

I then have them repeat the exercise imagining they are back when they made their foundational career decisions (often in their early 20s), and where they might see their priorities 10 or 20 years in the future. For many, this exercise is eye-opening—many find that the career they chose was once the right fit, but they hadn't adapted their careers to new realities. It also jumpstarts their thinking about how they might adjust their careers while considering the trade-offs involved. According to one dad who assessed his priorities and changed his career:

> *When I turned 40, I looked at my life and how it would fit with being the kind of father I wanted to be. After lots of thought and discussion with my wife, I stepped off the C-level ladder and found a more lifestyle-friendly path. I always wanted to be a hands-on dad and be there in ways many dads aren't able to. Now, I am that dad for my two*

*girls—picking them up at school and taking them to
tennis lessons, fixing dinner, and reading to them.
So, I guess my experience shows you can make mid-
career changes, even if they are scary and difficult
and involve risk and luck.*

After thinking through priorities, if you discover a
mismatch, you might want to shift your career to uncover more time for life and fatherhood. A benefit of
being in the harvesting phase is that you have leverage
to take charge of your career. You likely have a wide network and a good reputation and are able to explore different employers and roles. Perhaps equally important,
you may have power to renegotiate the terms of your current situation.

If you are open to rethinking your career to make
time to be a more present father, there are many paths
to consider. You may not need to change as much as you
think to have a big impact on your work and life. Sometimes a mindset change is enough. Look for opportunities to change within your current role first, and if bigger
changes are needed, expand outward from there.

Get Over Yourself

In her book about career downshifting, Amy Saltzman
concludes that the greatest barrier is often one's ego.[3]

"Getting over the idea that they will be cast as failures is the greatest challenge facing downshifters . . . stepping back is often the culmination of a painful battle between personal needs and professional expectations," Saltzman says. This dad's dilemma illustrates her point:

> *I had a reputation as a workhorse—I was the guy that would work until he dropped to get the job done. After my son was born, I wanted to spend more time at home and be an active part of family life. So, I decided I would leave the office at 3:30 two days a week, do dinner, bath, and bedtime stories with my son, then log back in at 8 p.m. to finish my workday . . . But what would other people think? Was my "workhorse" reputation going to suffer? I found myself yearning to justify and explain myself, even though no one had said one word to me about my new schedule.*

It takes a strong sense of self to revisit a successful career by considering changes that might better correspond to the full range of our priorities.

Explore Flexible and Remote Work

Covid-19 transformed the workplace. Many formerly resistant companies now allow and even embrace remote work. This opens many possibilities for you to negotiate for more flexibility at your current position. You may prefer a formal flex policy or simply more autonomy over where and when you work. You have an even stronger negotiating position if you have a successful track record of working from home during the pandemic.

Avoiding even a few commutes per week saves time and money, and work from home enables you to be flexible around family events (plus you are always home in time for dinner). Many firms now recruit outside their local areas, opening up more possibilities for you both in terms of finding employment and in your ability to relocate somewhere with a lower cost of living.

Prioritize Father-Friendly Employers

If options in your current role won't allow you the flexibility you're looking for, investigate employers with reputations for supporting their employees' life priorities. The *Fortune* 100 List, Glassdoor, the Fatherly 50 Best Companies for Working Fathers, and *Working Mother Magazine's* Best Employer lists can all be valuable resources. People in your network can provide valuable insight about cultural fit. Finally, no matter where you might apply or interview, ask questions about how their organization supports working parents, and whether they embrace whole-person workplace values.[4]

Consider Different Industry Sectors

Similar jobs at different employers can have very different work cultures and time demands. For instance, shareholder-oriented, publicly traded companies often exhibit high-pressure, "all in" work environments and less job security. Partnerships and privately held firms often take a longer-term view when it comes to employee matters. Public and not-for-profit sectors generally cannot match the pay offered by for-profit firms but try to make up for this with greater flexibility. For example, an auditing position at a Big Four accounting firm probably has more intensive time demands than an auditing position for a state government agency. Trading regular hours for lower salary may be a welcome career shift for you.

Recognize and Adjust to Financial Trade-Offs

Career paths that allow you to be more present at home usually come with lowered career trajectories and less income. To choose such a path, you and your spouse need to assess the financial consequences and ensure that your family is still well taken care of. This requires a hard look at your financial situation and may mean simplifying and cutting back significantly. You'll need to have honest family discussions, as options may affect your spouse's career; big expenses like housing, childcare, and college tuition; and your ability to afford family vacations and extracurriculars. Everyone needs to be on board. In my experience, many families are happy to cut back if it means more quality time with a less-stressed-out dad.

The men profiled in this article demonstrate that the best way out of a working dad's career trap is to take stock of your career path, assess whether your career fits well with being the father you want to be, and take steps, large or small, to align your career choices with your priorities.

Mastering the Dad Transition

by Bruce Feiler

Quick Takes

- Accept that becoming a father brings a host of emotions
- Find appropriate venues to explore your feelings
- Free yourself from old expectations
- Create new habits at home and embrace a new culture at work
- Update your life story to include the new chapter of fatherhood

Among the transitions people face in their lives, becoming a parent may be the most consequential. The fact that this life change is often expected and joyful does little to reduce the emotional upheaval and personal and professional adjustment required.

But while the transition that new moms face—everything from postpartum depression and career anxiety to a heightened sense of pride and purpose—has been deeply studied by academics and oft discussed in popular culture, the transition that new dads face has been woefully ignored by researchers and reduced to little more than a punchline in popular culture.

Yet the two transitions can't be separated. The impact brought on by massive growth in the number of working moms is inextricably entangled with the impact of having a new culture of engaged dads. As more and more moms have entered the workspace (two-thirds of mothers with children under six work outside the home; for those with children over six, the number balloons to 77%), more dads have entered the parenting space.[1]

Some of this change is by necessity—working moms, by definition, have less time in their day for childcare and increasingly demand that dads step up—but far more of the change is by choice. Dads, it turns out, enjoy being more involved in child-rearing. Asked how they view their role in the family, three-quarters of fathers say their role is "both earning money and caring for my child."

While this flowering of interest in fatherhood has many upsides for dads, moms, and children alike, it raises a host of complications and awkward adjustments for everyone involved, including employers and managers. And though the research into these questions does not go back decades, it has accelerated in recent years.

My own research into life transitions has found that they involve three phases. The first is what I call the "long goodbye," in which the person going through the transition mourns the life they're leaving behind. The second is the "messy middle," in which the person sheds certain habits, mindsets, and lifestyles and begins to create new ones. The third is the "new beginning," in which the person introduces their new self. These phases parallel nicely with the challenges and opportunities new fathers face.

Here, based on this growing body of knowledge, are five tips for new dads to make the transition into working fatherhood a process that's not just life disrupting, but life affirming, too.

Paternity Leave Resources on HBR.org

Paternity leave policies differ from country to country and company to company—and the policies are always changing. Rather than trying to describe all of these situations, we've chosen in this book to focus on more universal aspects of working fatherhood. If you are expecting a baby soon, HBR's website has many articles about how to prepare for paternity leave, what to do during it, and best practices for when you return to work. We recommend visiting HBR.org and searching for articles on "paternity leave" or "parental leave" to find the pieces that are most relevant to you.

—The Editors

1. Accept It

The first lesson for new dads is not to skip over the changes involved. A phase of life has passed. Instead, accept that becoming a father brings with it a host of emotions. These emotions include not just upbeat ones, like joy, elation, and pride, but also downbeat ones, like fear, anxiety, and helplessness.

Researchers in Australia did a comprehensive analysis of more than 500 research papers and found that anxiety disorders in expectant fathers begin in early pregnancy and are widespread across the perinatal period.[2] These feelings crest around birth, when dads often succumb to bouts of helplessness and solitude.[3] For men who already have a history of mental health challenges, these changes can be especially acute.[4]

On top of those emotions at home, dads often feel a sense of concern about falling behind or losing pace at work. Certain routines with colleagues and bosses, from social gatherings to conventions to weekend rounds of golf, may diminish in priority, thereby stoking fears that the responsibilities at home are undermining opportunities at work.

The point is that transitioning to fatherhood is an emotional experience; take time to identify and accept it.

2. Mark It

So how should working dads cope with these feelings?

The answer is to bring the feelings into the open by finding appropriate venues to explore them. My research has found that people use a variety of techniques to respond to the rush of emotions in life transitions: Some write about their feelings; others buckle down and push through. But 80% of people use rituals—public, often shared experiences that indicate to themselves and those around them that they're going through an emotional time and are preparing for what comes next.

The same applies to fathers. For those having a hard time adjusting to the sometimes abstract news of impending parenthood, for instance, the first sonogram has been found to be a galvanizing moment. While the new mom experiences the physical transformation, the dad sometimes needs the visual ritual.

A host of research has also shown that for working dads, sharing stories with others in a support group can help.[5] Even online groups work.[6] The reason such encounters are effective is that gathering with peers in safe settings allows new fathers to normalize their concerns and even use humor to exert some control over them. Expressing these feelings has been shown to lead to completeness, maturity, personal growth, and pride.

The success of such support groups led the Boston College Center for Work & Family to recommend that companies start fathers' affinity groups or offer brown-bag seminars targeted at men as a way to foster acceptance of the dual roles of working dads.[7]

3. Shed It

If the first phase of a life transition is focused on saying goodbye to a past that is not coming back, the second phase, "the messy middle," is concentrated on settling in and adjusting to the new reality. The first step in that process involves giving up old ways.

For working dads, this step means freeing yourself from expectations about your own identity, your relationship with your partner, even your job. A comprehensive study by two scholars in Brazil found that fathers in transition must learn to adjust in four key areas: (1) the father with himself; (2) the father with the mother and the baby; (3) the father with their support network; and (4) the father with his work.

The key finding: Fathers must not over-rely on their own fathers as role models, because previous generations of men were less focused on childrearing and balancing work and family. Instead, new fathers must shed these outdated expectations and turn instead to fathers of their own generation who are forging a new set of expectations, habits, and priorities.

Your role model as a working father is more likely to be a colleague or a friend—seek one out.

4. Create It

So what does this new generation of dads want?

The answer to that question may be the most exciting aspect of the working-dad transition. Dads today want a culture, both at home and at work, that embraces hands-on fatherhood. This desire reflects my own research into life transitions, when after saying goodbye to the past and shedding outdated patterns, people in the messy middle turn to astonishing acts of creativity.

In the case of working dads, that means creating new habits at home, from bonding with your baby to coordinating with your partner about what parts of childcare you'll take the lead on. It also means creating a new culture at work that embraces working dads. Make no mistake: Most dads enjoy returning to work. Yet research shows that 98% of them fear losing contact with their babies.

How new dads avoid that fate is by embracing new schedules and new ways of working. More than 75% of dads use flextime when available, 57% work from home at least some of the time (a number that will surely grow as working from home becomes even more prevalent in the wake of the coronavirus pandemic), and 27% use compressed workweeks.[8]

If you're a new dad *and* a manager, take advantage of these programs as a way of helping to normalize and routinize these accommodations and forge a new culture of fatherhood for future generations. As the researchers from Boston College put it: "Offering fathers (and all employees) the time to attend to their personal needs does not offer employees permission to 'slack off.' What it does do is permit them to be more focused and energized when they are working."

5. Tell It

The final phase of a life transition is the "new beginning"; it's the one that arrives at a critical time, when the elation of new fatherhood has passed and the reality of being a dad settles in. The most important skill in this stage: updating the story of your life to include the new chapter of fatherhood.

A life transition is fundamentally a narrative event in which we revisit and update our life story to accommodate a critical change. In this case, becoming a new dad is not just a temporary transition, but a permanent one. And it's not one that ends after a few months, but gets repeated over and over, as a child enters new phases and brings out new responsibilities, as future children come along and tax routines that were already hard won, as new responsibilities accrue at work and pull fathers away from family milestones, and as growing families require big moves, big purchases, and big challenges.

Life transitions are a lifetime sport, and fatherhood just may be the excuse you've long needed to start learning how to play it. But once you do, you'll find that the skills you master are applicable across your life. They can help you turn times that at first seemed overwhelming into times that are filled with affection, wonder, and discovery.

8

When Your Boss Doesn't Respect Your Family Commitments

by Rebecca Knight

Quick Takes

- Have a one-on-one conversation with your boss
- Frame your plans in terms of achieving their goals
- Communicate often—but set clear boundaries
- Find allies inside your organization
- Set aside time for yourself
- Be ready to move on if necessary

When trying to balance your work and family commitments, it helps to have a boss who is understanding and supportive: someone who doesn't raise an eyebrow when you sign off early to attend a school event or take a personal day to accompany an aging parent to a doctor's appointment.

But what if your manager isn't sympathetic to your familial responsibilities? Or worse, your boss is outright dismissive or is even hostile toward your obligations? How should you handle a boss who refuses to acknowledge the other demands on your time? How can you find room for flexibility? What should you say about your family commitments? And who should you turn to for moral and professional support?

What the Experts Say

Too many working parents and other employees with extensive caregiving responsibilities have stories of a manager who gives them an assignment at 4 p.m. and asks for it the next morning, or a boss who makes disparaging comments about another working parent who doesn't seem loyal to the company. "There are some managers who are unsympathetic to the challenges their employees face at home and some who intentionally turn a blind eye," says Avni Patel Thompson, the founder and CEO of Modern Village, a company that provides technology solutions for parents. "Other managers may have positive intent but lack empathy or ideas on how to [support their employees]."

When you work for a manager who doesn't recognize your family obligations, your strategy must be multifaceted, says Ella F. Washington, professor at Georgetown University's McDonough School of Business and a consultant and coach at Ellavate Solutions. You need to figure out how to productively navigate the situation with your boss, while also collaborating with your colleagues and family to create a schedule and "set boundaries" that work for everyone. The goal is to "try to get your boss to meet you halfway," she says. Here are some ideas.

Know your rights

First, "know your rights" and understand what you're entitled to in terms of paid leave and care options, says Thompson. Do some research into your company's policies and whether there are alternative work arrangements on offer. An increasing number of organizations have instituted flexible work plans for employees, and many states have flex-work policies in place for their government workers. Washington recommends talking to your company's HR person, too, if you have one, to learn what options and accommodations are available to you. "Knowledge is power," she says.

Be up front about your personal situation

Next, have a one-on-one conversation with your boss in which you are "honest and transparent about your limitations," says Thompson. Make clear your commitment to the company and your team, but also explain the additional responsibilities outside of work. After all, your manager's lack of sympathy is likely not malicious, but thoughtless. For instance, if your boss doesn't have children, they may be aware of the "superficial or obvious" tasks related to remote learning but oblivious to the fact that parents are also serving as their kids' tech support, math tutors, writing coaches, and line cooks, says Thompson. They may not realize why a conversation with your child's teacher or guidance counselor has to take place during work hours, rather than early morning or in the evening. Explaining this to your boss may not be an easy conversation, but don't let your discomfort cause you to avoid the subject. "Silence is what makes managers nervous," warns Thompson. Remember, too, you're not throwing a woe-is-me pity party, says Washington. "This isn't about making excuses"—you're stating facts. Your tone should exude confidence and commitment.

Exhibit empathy

Next, summon compassion. It's not easy to be a boss. Many managers are under pressure. "They're stressed, anxious, and struggling to do more with less," says Washington. Consider the situation from their perspective.

Thompson says your empathy should be both "genuine and strategic." Ask your manager about their pain points. Find out where their worries lie. Be sincere—show you care about them as a human being—and be tactical. Ask about their "objectives and the metrics they need to hit," she says. "You'll get important information about what they're concerned about" that will help you sharpen your focus in terms of the work you prioritize.

Have a plan—or two or three

Once you "understand what's top of mind" for your manager, you can frame your plans for getting your job done in a way that helps them achieve their goals and objectives, says Thompson. Focus on results. When you're a caregiver, your schedule can often be unpredictable, so it's important to make a plan as well as several contingency ones. Address your manager's "insecurities about you not pulling your weight" by demonstrating that you're "making arrangements to get your work done." You want your manager to come away from your conversations thinking, "They've got this."

Don't be shy about reminding your manager of your track record for delivering on expectations, adds Washington. "Your past performance is the strongest indicator of your future performance," she says. Hopefully, your manager will come to see "that what's most important is not *how* the job gets done, but that it gets done."

Communicate often

Always keep your boss in the loop, says Washington. If you're not in the office, you might consider "instituting a daily check-in" or at least providing an email update every few days. "Your objective is to make your manager feel comfortable that the work is getting done," she says.

This communication doesn't require more face time though. Instead of a status update conference call, you could write an email to your team that lays out "your objectives for the week and gives visibility to what you're working on." Or in place of a team meeting on Zoom, encourage your colleagues to "collaborate on Slack," which allows you to "fire off messages even while your kids are sitting next to you."

Articulate boundaries

If your boss is a face-time tyrant, it can be tough to establish boundaries, but it's still important to do. We all need time in our day that's off-limits for work, says Washington. "If 6 p.m. is when you have dinner and put the kids down," so be it. "Have those boundaries—and let your boss know that you will be unavailable then."

But if your manager continues to be disrespectful of your family time, you need to have a conversation. Frame the discussion around you—how you prefer to structure your workday and how and when you perform best. Explain that you need your nonwork hours to regroup and take care of your family commitments. Without that time away from work, you will not be able to fully devote yourself to your job.

Broaden your network

If your direct boss continues to be difficult about your family commitments, make a concerted effort to find allies within your organization, says Thompson. These allies might include peers, colleagues in different departments, and managers outside your division. "Build relationships with people who see you for the whole life that you have," says Thompson. "That way, if down the line, things get contentious [with your boss], you've got options."

In addition to broadening your professional network, allies offer moral support, says Washington. Talk to your colleagues and find out how they're balancing their jobs with their caregiving responsibilities. "Find out how others are making this work," she says.

Take care of yourself

Working for someone who doesn't respect your life outside of work can be exhausting, so make sure you're taking time for yourself. Be purposeful about giving yourself "a forced mental break," says Thompson. Make time to read, cook, dance, run, meditate—or any other activity that you enjoy or helps you relax. "Schedule joy," she says.

And even if exercise isn't usually your thing, Thompson suggests finding time for it every day, especially during this difficult period. "Don't underestimate the power of 20–30 minutes of daily physical activity," she says. At a time when your boss is being difficult and "nothing feels in your control," getting your endorphins pumping should be a priority.

Bide your time

Even with your best efforts, the situation may not improve. In this case, Thompson's recommendation is to be the best employee you can be under the circumstances. "Make sure you deliver on expectations," she says. "Don't give your boss any ammunition" against you. Your boss might never be empathetic to your personal situation, says Washington. "If you're not getting support and the organization is not being inclusive of your needs, maybe this work environment isn't the best for your career development," she says. It may be time to move on.

Adapted from "When Your Boss Doesn't Respect Your Family Commitments," on hbr.org, September 1, 2020 (product #H05UK1).

Why Dads Need Parenting Allies at Work

by Han-Son Lee and Hugh Wilson

Quick Takes

- Find allies among fathers and mothers—both new and experienced parents
- Speak openly about your life as a parent to make more connections
- Join existing conversations around parenting
- Create a dads' network at your company

We have all heard the truism that it takes a village to raise a child, and of course we all know that if you want to get ahead at work and in your career, you need to be an effective teammate and successful networker. But most fathers have not yet put two and two together and realized the importance of making parenting allies at work.

Parenting allies can provide emotional support, ideas, and a sounding board that dads are otherwise missing at work. Together, a group of allies can bring collective pressure to achieve a culture of work-life balance in which fathers are more involved in the everyday lives of their children.

Your allies will often be other parents, mothers as well as fathers. Moms have been fighting for parental work rights for decades, and they'll appreciate the vigor a new generation of involved dads can bring to the movement.

Moving beyond the "traditional" dad, together

Our research on modern working dads shows that while fathers still want (and need) successful careers, they also want to be present and involved as parents and partners.[1] They want to share the workload and the joys. They want to soothe a crying baby in the night and be home in time for baths and story time. They want fulfilling weekends of family time and meaningful interactions with their children throughout the week.

Unfortunately, policy and tradition are still holding dads back in the workplace. The notion of fatherhood being segregated from work life has been the norm since the advent of the office. Western corporate culture has always valued presenteeism and face time. Rather than put up a fight against this culture, many dads succumb to it, particularly if their finances are fragile. "Dads feel greater pressure to provide for and support their family—and more so if their spouses' careers and wages have taken a hit when children come along," says Vicki Psarias, author of *Mumboss* and founder of Honest Mum. "[It] has a knock-on effect on both partners." Mothers end up losing out in the office, fathers end up losing out at home, and the cycle perpetuates.

More and more dads want to unshackle themselves from limited and joyless notions of traditional fatherhood, but many have realized that their employers—and often their colleagues—will not be naturally inclined to consider their role as fathers. If they want change, it's up to them to fight for it.

Forming parenting alliances

It's a cliché that many men willingly buy into the notion that stoicism is strength, and emotion a weakness. While sometimes true, numerous studies have shown that while women prefer to work in teams, men prefer to work alone. Men don't naturally nurture alliances because men are less natural team players.

But if you're hoping to effect real change, going it alone is a recipe for failure. Think of a group advocating for healthier options in the work canteen. Alone, only one individual is screaming into the wind about the need for a salad bar. With allies, that person becomes one voice among many, spread across the organization, discussing the well-being and productivity gains that healthier lunch options would bring. Before you know it, it's no longer about one person's desire for salad, but about the benefits to the bottom line of reduced sick days and the uptick in retention rates that results from taking staff well-being seriously. Allies widen the discussion and take it in different directions. They have conversations with a wider range people. They normalize the ideas.

Now think about advocating for a more progressive paternity policy. One dad can't fight for this alone—he needs allies to help spread the word. A preponderance of conversations are needed about how better leave means happier, more productive dads.[2] Fathers, and those who may become fathers, stay with the company, and new talent is easier to recruit. What a business loses in long hours, it gains in loyalty. These messages need to spread across the shop floor, in HR, marketing, and finance, and in the CEO's office.

So who can be a parenting ally? More people than you might think. They're likely to be parents, but not necessarily young ones. Older moms and dads who remember the challenges they faced combining parenthood and careers can be a great source of information and advocacy.

An ally can have any job title, though it's preferable if they either have a direct influence on parental policy at work or have helped put parenting policies into practice. They come in all shapes and sizes. They can be sounding boards for your own thoughts or ideas, or they can be in a position to spread those ideas widely. Allies aren't *just* for advocacy. They might have your back when you have to rush home to look after a sick child or offer a sympathetic ear when you're overwhelmed. If they can support you emotionally or practically—and you do the same for them—they're a worthy ally.

Start a parental conversation at work

So how does all this begin? I often hear of dads who are successful and popular at work and who keep the fatherhood side of their identities entirely hidden from colleagues and/or clients alike.[3] The way to overcome this reticence is to simply start talking about being a dad, in all its messy, wonderful glory. Talk about your weekend and include the family outing. Mention the fact that you're leaving on time today to get home for story time. Joke about that diaper change that went horribly wrong.

Start to normalize your parenting life, and your colleagues will see you don't treat it as a taboo subject. Maybe a parent with younger children will want to ask you for advice or a parent of older kids will want to give you some. Either way, you've created a space for discussion. If you're a manager, you've also provided an example for other dads to talk about their lives as parents. Don't forget to mention the pressure of your dual responsibilities. Free others to admit that being a good worker and a good dad is sometimes a tough balancing act.

If you work remotely, you won't bump into other parents in the kitchen, but the principle remains the same, even if you're chatting over Zoom or Teams. Hang your children's artwork in your background. Make your profile photo a family photo. Take an occasional meeting with a toddler on your lap. Start a Slack group for parents and parenting issues, invite a few people, and watch word of mouth take over. Create a virtual conversation around parenting.

Join existing conversations

Once you start talking, you probably won't stop, because you'll find that more conversations are going on around work and parenting than you imagined.

Some of these will be informal chats among close colleagues. But there may also be formal parents' groups in your organization. These are a brilliant way for moms and dads to start talking about the issues at work that affect them as parents. I've led a number of parent networking sessions where I've been asked to talk about the challenges I've faced as a working dad.

Workplace parenting groups are more likely to be mom-focused, but only because moms tend to set them up. Virginia Herlihy, founder and CEO of the organizational change company How Do You Do It, urges men to join in. Involved dads, she says, "are the allies who have the potential to make the biggest difference for working moms, who have trodden this pathway before them but who need to be joined on it by dads in order to give both parents real choices about who does what at work and home."

Create your own dads' network

If there are no ready-made parent networks at your workplace, start your own. Make it a dads' network, at least to start with, to coax reluctant fathers out into the open. Some men might be put off by the idea of a general parenting club and more comfortable discussing issues with other dads. You can change the policy, if that feels right, over time. I've seen more and more work-based dad clubs starting to emerge, not least through our own Dad Connect program, which aims to help dads forge connections within and across organizations.[4]

Ask other dads at your workplace if they'd like to meet informally to talk about issues around parenthood and work that are important to them. It shouldn't require too much time or energy, so once a month at lunchtime might be enough to begin. Ask HR if you can advertise the group in the staff newsletter or put a poster on the notice board. Keep an email list or Slack group of interested individuals and contact them before each meeting.

As the group becomes more established, widen its responsibilities. Invite a member of the senior management team to talk about what the business is doing to promote family-friendly working practices. Invite moms to meetings or create ties with mom groups in the business. Compile a document of innovations the group would like to see implemented, alongside examples of best practice. Keep the group engaged between meetings through regular messaging and encourage members to discuss practical, everyday questions, like recommendations for family-friendly restaurants or the best things to do with a 4-year-old this weekend.

Those are just a few ideas. What you do with your allies is up to you. Whether in a formal or informal setting, and whether you're having the conversation with dads, moms, or everyone, the most important thing is to start the conversation. That is the first small step toward a more progressive vision of parenting and work. The more people who take part in the debate, the harder it becomes to ignore, and the sooner we'll achieve truer gender equality at work.

How to Identify a Family-Friendly Employer

by Suzanne Brown

Quick Takes

- Browse the company website
- Read any public information and reviews
- Talk to past employees in your network
- Ask about a typical day in your interviews
- Discuss flexibility and remote work
- Ask HR about benefits and support options

f you're a working parent looking for a new job or interested in making a career move, your search might not only be about finding a great professional opportunity. You may also want a more family-friendly employer. If that's the case, it's helpful to get a more complete picture of work life at the potential employer *before* you come on board. Learning how the company has supported other parents will help you understand if its actions and culture align with what you want and need.

Before you even explore potential employers, identify what you're looking for. This gives you the lens through which you look at a job opening, so you can start to understand if this organization can give you the opportunity and lifestyle that you want. Think through the most important commitments you have with your family that might impact time at work, like eating dinner as a family each night, coaching your child's soccer team, or assisting with remote schoolwork. Consider what benefits you want from the employer and how important they are to you and your family. Reflect on how your current or previous employers have fallen short, to identify what was missing. It could also be helpful to visualize your ideal scenario as a working parent both today and long term as your kids get older or your family grows.

Then, as opportunities present themselves and you line up interviews, do your homework. You may feel limited, especially if you're stuck interviewing remotely or unable to see office culture firsthand, but you can find a lot of information—as well as ask a lot of questions—to find the right opportunity. Here's how.

Online Resources

Start with the company website. Review how the company talks about employees and what it shares regarding employee support. Creating an environment for working parents begins at the top. Look at senior leadership and the company's board of directors. Can you tell if they have families? Do they talk about a family-friendly environment? Are there women? If you're answering no to most of these questions, this may not be a family-friendly environment, especially at more senior levels, which could be a red flag for your long-term growth opportunities.

Look, too, for any information about employee resource groups (ERGs), paying special attention to those for working moms and dads. Review any public information on family leave, if a child were to become ill, a spouse or partner required assistance after an injury, or an aging parent needed care. Dig into any parental leave and programs offered to new moms, such as a part-time ramp-up or a work-from-home period, to see if they extend these options to new dads, as well.

Wherever the company features employees on the website, such as in published articles, on its blog, or in press releases, look for information on a typical day in the office that suggests a reasonable work life, or signals that colleagues and the company as a whole have positively impacted employees' work life or family. (Accounting firm DHG, for instance, features such stories on its corporate blog.) Then, see how their stories compare to what else you find on the website.

Go outside the company's website, too. Do a quick online search for recent news, both good and bad. Read current and former employee reviews on places like Glassdoor and review top 100 lists in publications such as those published in *Working Mother.* And track down interviews with senior leaders to see what they share about their family life.

Personal Connections

In addition to online resources, tap into your network to get personal anecdotes about the company. You want to piece together a more complete picture of being a working parent with this employer. You might see warning signs or get ideas for questions to ask during interviews.

Use LinkedIn and Facebook to find friends, friends of friends, connections through your professional network, or school alumni who may be employed, or previously employed, by the company. Talk to them about company culture and probe about official policy versus reality. If these are former employees, don't be afraid to ask about why they left.

Talk to them about work-life balance failures, as well. Keep an ear out for statements like, "Too many moms are put on a 'mommy track'" or "All the working dads end up on the same team." Perhaps the company tried a program to support working parents, and it didn't work. What did the company learn? What can you uncover about why working parents leave? Is there a consistent pattern of working parents leaving because they lack support?

Interviews with Current Team Members

When you reach the interview stage, ask about the position in question, but also aim to find out more about the company and its culture. Consider who is interviewing you and listen closely to what they share. If all of your interviewers say they don't have a family or they have kids and a full-time, stay-at-home spouse or caretaker, this could be a red flag.

This is a great opportunity to hear about a typical day, too. Pay attention to the length of a normal workday and if there are back-to-back meetings or video calls, all day, every day. This could hint at long hours or an expectation to work late nights or early mornings.

Another great topic to cover in your interviews is flexibility. Look for formal structures such as job shares, part-time options, split schedules, and day-to-day flexibility for when your child gets sick, has a school event, or requires your attention while you work from home. Covid-19 shifted how employers approach flexibility, especially remote work.[1] Ask about their experience during the pandemic. How did managers and the employer support employees who were supervising their children's distance learning or entertaining young children? Are flexibility and remote work now built into the work culture—or was that considered temporary? And remember that being family friendly extends beyond managing work life with your children. Find out how this employer supports families with aging parents and sick family members as well.

If you have specific questions about benefits, talk to your HR contact. Ask about the benefits and support structures for working parents. These benefits could include paying to transport milk for moms who pump while traveling or for backup childcare and elderly care.

And inquire about workplace wellness programs that help prevent things like burnout.

Choosing the right position is not only about checking the role for the right fit; you want the company to be the right fit, too. Tap into the many resources available early on and during the interview process to uncover red flags and do research to understand how work life will be with a new employer. There are many family-friendly organizations. Take the time to fully understand the opportunity on both professional and personal levels before you sign on.

Adapted from content posted on hbr.org, September 8, 2020 (product #H05UAQ).

When a Stay-at-Home Dad Goes Back to Work

by Whitney Johnson and Roger Johnson

Quick Takes

- Plan your workforce reentry before you exit
- Embrace adaptation and change
- Men's networks tilt toward other men—use this to your advantage
- When you do relaunch, be an example for other dads

n 2015, our family upended itself and moved from Boston, our home of nearly 15 years, to central Virginia so Roger could accept a position at Southern Virginia University, an up-and-coming liberal arts university.

Nearly a decade earlier, with a PhD in molecular biology from Columbia University, he was pursuing a promising career as an assistant professor at University of Massachusetts Medical School and had recently published a paper in *Nature*. Our children were eight and four, and Whitney was constantly traveling for business. We decided that our children needed more parental involvement, a scenario faced by many dual-career couples.

So Roger paused his career to become a stay-at-home dad. In 2016, only about 24% of the roughly 2 million stay-at-home fathers in the U.S. were home to care for their children; the rest were home for other reasons.[1] It's a small club.

Our children benefited tremendously—and of course Whitney did, too. Roger, frazzled from the solo juggling of work and family during my frequent business trips, was relieved to put family first, a closely held value.

What didn't benefit was his career.

When we were ready for him to on-ramp, as Sylvia Ann Hewlett calls it, we found that men returning to work face different obstacles. For women, relaunching is tough but increasingly doable—the path may be arduous, but at least it is well-trodden. A woman's sabbatical for family reasons can be explained, and such leaves of absence are comprehensible if still disadvantageous. But for men, there effectively is no path. Some of our biases about gender roles are stubbornly persistent. People think there must be something wrong with a man who leaves his career to rear his children; they wonder if he's hiding something, or least think there might be more to the story.

In fact, during his first year as a stay-at-home father, Roger's colleagues were incredulous. Was he really leaving? Or just looking for a new opportunity? Job offers appeared out of nowhere. He declined them repeatedly.

Seven years later, with our kids in middle school and high school, Roger started to make inquiries, still believing he was marketable. His superb credentials didn't garner even a nibble, except for the suggestion that he try volunteer work. It was discouraging, depressing. Beyond the perceived oddness of his career hiatus, academia, with its tenure track, is not especially friendly to career interruptions. He nearly gave up, thinking his career was over.

But in 2015, with our oldest child graduating from high school, he doubled down, tapped into his network, and got a shot at teaching biology, chemistry, and bio-chemistry at Southern Virginia University. If he'd stayed in the workforce originally, his path would have led him in the direction of research. Now he's focused on teaching and aiding the entrepreneurial effort to expand this small university. He loves the classroom, where there is potential for both career and personal development. In the academic world, focusing on teaching is seen as a step back, but to Roger, his new job became a promising step, with new space to grow and flourish.

Because Whitney is self-employed now, she can live and work anywhere. That's a luxury she wouldn't have enjoyed earlier in her career—when working on Wall Street, for instance, not only because finance requires a foothold in New York or London, but also because in those years there wasn't sophisticated technology to facilitate working remotely. It is impossible to overstate how these technological developments have expanded the choices available to many working couples. Now, the question was never, *would* we move to Virginia to accept Roger's opportunity? The question was, *how could we not* do so?

The dilemmas faced by dual-career couples involve trade-offs—often very difficult ones. It is usually only as we pursue a particular path that we discover all the challenges. They are largely opaque at the start of the journey, and they vary depending on situational specifics. But here are a few things we've learned from our experience that may be helpful to other couples who consider this option:

First, it's more difficult to on-ramp in some professions than others. Roger's field is science, which is always rapidly evolving. And academia, as noted, doesn't make this easy either. Carol Fishman Cohen, cofounder of iRelaunch, has a lot of experience with on-rampers and emphasized this: "I had seen thousands of relaunches, but only four into tenure-track positions. [Roger] was the the fifth." In many fields of endeavor, we can quickly become dated and left behind. Regardless of your industry, plan your workforce reentry—including how to remain current in your discipline—before you exit, especially if you plan to be out for more than a year.

Second, although Roger's gender seemed to be an impediment to on-ramping—since stay-at-home dads are still a rarity—we did see some specific advantages from it. A man's professional network, if cultivated and maintained, seems to provide avenues back into a career that are often more helpful than those enjoyed by women. Our networks tend to tilt toward our own gender, and men are more likely to be in positions of influence in organizations. In contrast, women seem to have less ability to give other women a leg up (research backs this up, and unfortunately the same is true for people of color).[2] Perhaps that won't be true for you, but it has been true in our experience.

Third, attention has been directed toward the impact of income inequity on the male ego, but the bigger challenge may be adjusting to the loss of a "work" identity. This can be difficult for anyone, but for men the effect may be amplified. It can take an emotional toll that shouldn't be underestimated. And a stay-at-home dad won't have the same network of support that stay-at-home moms may be able to develop. Whitney has a huge network of women who are lead parents, but for a variety of reasons, that wasn't a network Roger could plug into.

Fourth, while mothers are often portrayed as doing "the hardest job in the world" or "the most important job there is," fathers are more likely to be portrayed as incompetent buffoons who can't figure out how to change a diaper or dress their children properly. Some of this comes from women, some from other dads, and some from the media. But fathers who take primary responsibility for the care of their children make important contributions—they shouldn't be mocked or emasculated. No one benefits from a dialogue that demeans the work of anyone who chooses to be a career parent.

Fifth, when you do relaunch, talk about it. Says Fishman Cohen, "Part of the problem is there are not enough examples of men returning to work after years away. One of our priorities at iRelaunch is to feature hundreds of return-to-work success stories in our articles and on our website. However, we have trouble getting men to go on record when they successfully return. They keep telling us they would rather everyone forget they ever took a career break in the first place. That shows the stigma is still alive and well. As more men take career breaks for care-giving reasons and then successfully relaunch careers, I expect this will change."

For every family, there are multiple roles to be filled. As couples—whether they're dual-career, career/job, career/stay-at-home, off-ramped, on-ramped, or otherwise—we divide and conquer depending on our respective circumstances. Perhaps the key to success is adaptability—being able to invent and reinvent, shifting priorities as needed within the constant context of satisfying both our personal and familial needs and ambitions.

Adapted from "What It's Like When a Stay-at-Home Dad Goes Back to Work," on hbr.org, April 19, 2016 (product #H02TF8).

Section 3

All Work and No Play . . .

Dedicating Time to Your Family and Yourself

Four Ways to Make More Time for Family

by James Sudakow

Quick Takes

- Make time for the little things

- Know what's truly urgent

- Make sure your colleagues respect your boundaries

- Set goals to be a better father and co-parent

- Make intentional decisions around work-life balance and follow through on them ike most of us, I think a lot about how to balance my duties at work with my responsibilities at home. I happen to be a husband and a dad raising four kids. My professional success shouldn't come at the expense of my family, nor should being present at home compromise my ability to run a business.

That's the work-life dilemma many parents face today. I felt it so strongly that I wrote a book about my experiences. But during that process, I kept hearing the same lingering question:

"Do dads actually care about work-life balance?"

According to the Boston College Center for Work & Family, one of the few organizations focusing on the changing role dads play both at home and in the workplace, the answer is a resounding yes. It recently found that fathers may experience as much or more work-family conflict than their female counterparts. Its study revealed that while 80% to 90% of millennial dads wanted career advancement, only 4% strongly agreed that they'd be willing to sacrifice personal and family time to achieve it.[1] The men surveyed rated work-life balance as the primary factor to consider when measuring success and as the third most important criteria for choosing a job. (For moms, it ranked first.)

So, what can fathers—from any generational cohort—who want to focus on both career and family do to get the balance right? I spoke with five men in top leadership roles who also have families about the advice they give the dads who work for them. Their titles vary: CEO, president, chief human resources officer, executive vice president or general manager, and executive director. They're in different stages of parenthood—one has three young kids, two have elementary-age kids, one has teenagers, and one has three grown kids. Four common themes emerged from all my conversations.

Make time for the little things

Birthdays, holidays, graduations, trips to Disneyland—many leaders suggest that being present for those events is enough to constitute work-life balance. But the men I spoke with described these big things as just "table stakes." In their view, it's actually the myriad of little, day-to-day interactions that really matter. Car trips to the doctor, walks around the neighborhood, morning drives to school—these moments often yield the most important memories.

One dad who created time for his daughters in that way when they were young told me that he now feels like he has "a thousand mini YouTube videos [of them] running around in his head." He still prioritizes taking the girls to school every morning. And none of it has hurt his career. Instead, it allows him to be a leader without regret when he's at work.

Know what's truly urgent

Work can be urgent, and often for good reason. One leader told a story about a time early in his career when his kids were little. When he wasn't traveling, his nightly routine upon arriving home from work was to give them their baths and then put them to bed. He would then eat dinner by himself and go back to his email. His epiphany came when his wife "nicely chastised" him about this habit. It caused him to reflect about why he wasn't waiting until the next morning to return to work.

He realized that most of it could wait with no dire business consequences. He stresses that this isn't procrastination in disguise. He—and all the other leaders I spoke with—talked about how important appropriate urgency has been for their careers. But this "artificial urgency" is a significant barrier to achieving balance.

Set boundaries

Leadership roles can be all consuming. If you're in a top job, you've earned the privilege of being ultimately accountable, and you can't take a break from that. But the dads I spoke with all talked about setting boundaries. One made a point of coaching all three of his sons' sports teams. Another prioritized family dinners during the week, even though the company had a "work-late" and "face-time" culture.

The specifics of the rules these men set for themselves varied. What was consistent for all of them, though, was the intentionality. They were clear with their colleagues, ensuring that there would be consistent times when work and family could not intersect. Even though work could have easily slipped in, they were intentional about protecting those periods. In my book, I refer to it as "ruthless compartmentalization." For me, it means blocking out half-day segments during the week that are for my family and I do not take work calls or check email.

Set goals

All these dads spoke about consistency as a critical factor for success both at home and at work. At work, that means leading and managing their teams in a consistent way, meeting their stated business goals and commitments, hitting their key performance indicators. Most families don't have performance metrics. But you can create them for yourself to ensure that you're a better dad to your kids and a better co-parent to your spouse. It could be as simple as clarifying how many family dinners you are going to have each week, or how many school drop-offs you are going to do. I got very granular about these in my own life because it helped me figure out exactly how and where I wanted to spend the hours of each day.

One leader I spoke with—divorced and on his second marriage—lamented that his presence at home was inconsistent in his first marriage, and he attributes his divorce to that fact. He's made changes this time around. Specifically, he prioritizes taking calls from his kids over business calls and schedules key business meetings around his children's school calendar. Another told me that "the best job he ever had" forced him to travel coast to coast every week, but because that schedule made his home life too unpredictable, he gave it up for a different role that allowed him to be a more consistent presence at home. Yet another explained that being home more often allowed him to be a better disciplinarian. When he was there more sporadically, he wanted to be the fun parent; when he was around more, he felt better about being a more complete parent and enforcing rules.

When you look at all these stories together, the overriding message is clear: Fathers have to make intentional decisions around work-life balance and follow through on them. The outcome is a more fulfilled life as a parent and professional.

Adapted from "4 Ways Working Dads Can Make More Time for Family," on hbr.org, April 9, 2019.

Commit to a No-Work Weeknight

by Mark McCartney

Quick Takes

- Recognize that family time *is* recovery time for work

- Commit to at least one work-free night per week

- Use rituals to carve out and protect your family time

- The more structured a ritual is, the better it will stick

often tell the story of Mike, a coaching client of mine and head of sales at an aviation company in the United States. Once, he told me, on the first day of a holiday away, he announced to his wife and three children that he preferred being at work to being there with them. It happened when his wife told him to put his phone away at the breakfast table, but the root causes of his outburst were an always-on work culture combined with a toxic relationship with his boss in Paris. He was unable to rest even on holiday because, as he described it, it felt as if "there were always sharks under the surface which could bite him at any moment." Work was constantly close by, even though he was far away from his office on an island in the Indian Ocean. His wife was infuriated with his behavior because she had organized the holiday and had briefed her own colleagues only to contact her with urgent matters. Why couldn't he do the same? Didn't the kids deserve at least one week a year of their father's attention?

Mike was exhausted. He had not had an evening off from work for more than nine months. He thought this was a sign of commitment.

Few dads would ever say something like what Mike said, but what do your actions really show to your family? Do you find it impossible to detach from work during the week? Do you regularly work during what is supposed to be family time? Have you almost forgotten how to switch off? Rest assured, your partner and your children notice. Fortunately, there are practical steps that anyone—even the busiest and most ambitious among us—can do both to make more time for family and to make family time better for all.

Good for you, your family, and your employer

When I start with my clients, they often aren't yet ready to get to the practical question of *how* to spend more time with their families; they're still struggling with *why* it's important. Even as work and society are changing, old beliefs prevail—*being a successful provider means you're a successful father . . . hours are how you get ahead . . . time is money.* Seen through this lens, family time seems to be stealing hours you could be using to provide your children with a better life. But in fact, these thoughts aren't just outdated; they can actually be detrimental to performance at work. The twin pressures of professional life and parenting are a recipe for burnout.

An international rugby player I coached in a leadership program in France told me, "I used to get paid to recover, but now in business, time to recover is seen as time away from performing." Dads need to reframe their mindset about family time the way high-performance athletes do—it isn't just time spent away from work, it's time spent recovering *for* work. We must find simple ways to reduce the number of hours we work and embrace productivity instead of busyness.

The best place to start is one evening a week. Stefan, 43, father of two, head of data at a global pharmaceutical company, cooks dinner with his two daughters. It is the highlight of the week. Lively conversation fills the kitchen and delicious meals fill the stomachs. Stefan told me in one of our sessions, "I heard my daughter, Amy, tell a friend who came over that Tuesday was the best day of the week because she gets time with her dad and how much she loves choosing the recipes each week." There's simply no replacement for this kind of replenishment. Stefan, along with most of my coaching clients, attests that the workdays that follow family nights are his most productive each week. They are better able to focus on the priorities the next day. They sleep better, eat better, and drink less coffee.

What's more, breaking from our habitual ways of working provides useful insights that can help us at home and at work in surprising ways. Peter, a director at a U.K. utility company spends more time outside walking during the day partly as a result of going for a Wednesday walk with his 8-year-old daughter. As Peter told me, "I call it my time to walk things out . . . either with my daughter so I can fully listen to her or workwise to think through a challenge I am facing at work."

If you are still in doubt about the benefit of one non-work evening a week, talk to your most important stakeholder. One client, a high-flying lawyer, told me, "My wife is a clinician and when we asked our children what they most wanted for Christmas, they both said, unprompted, 'More time with you.'" Ask your children directly, "Would you like Dad to stop working earlier one evening a week so that we can enjoy some time together?" I think you know what they'll say.

Use rituals to carve out—and protect— your family time

We all know that simple declarations like "I'll spend more time with my family on weeknights" don't work. They're like New Year's resolutions that fade before February. My clients have their most success when they think in terms of *rituals*. Once established, rituals are hard to shift and provide vital structure and routine for the entire family.

I recommend starting with an effective, simple, and practical ritual you can introduce tomorrow: one or two no-work evenings per week.

The first step is anticipating the derailers to your new plan: your partner's work, children's evening activities, client expectations, unanticipated projects. Then you can agree with the family one nonwork evening a week. Many clients choose Wednesday as a halfway point in the workweek.

One simple way of turning this into a ritual is to use the if-X-then-Y rubric. *If* it is Wednesday, *then* I finish at 5 p.m. Once you have decided on the evening, tell those who need to know (family *and* work colleagues . . . even sometimes clients, providing a clear backup). Then, hold each other to account. No sneaky checking the phone under the kitchen table or ducking out of bedtime routines to finish off a task. If you're caught, there needs to be an agreed-upon consequence (your children will love this bit).

The more structure you can apply to a ritual, the better it will stick. Think about an activity you could schedule on your nonwork evening. Going for a family walk. Playing a board game. Picking a topic each week to talk about over dinner. One client cooked a meal from a different country each Tuesday with his 8-year-old son and called it "Round the World in 80 meals." In addition to eating a Nigerian peanut stew, they also learned about each country, resulting in a history, geography, and music lesson.

One or two evenings a week is just one step toward increased sustainability. Once a client has adopted this ritual as a habit, they often go on to apply the same approach to weekends (often Sunday) and to family holidays. Stefan pushes the ritual a few steps further: he encourages his team to take off one evening a week, too, resulting in new norms and higher engagement scores, and he clears the first 90 minutes of the day after an evening off since he knows that his focus and energy are at their height.

• • •

Mike, the dad who had the outburst on vacation, realized that work had intruded too far into family life. He was struggling at work, too; his advancement had stalled because his total focus on work was demotivating to the people he led. Our coaching sessions focused on these challenges. Once he had accepted that time off is not time wasted, he continued to make changes at work and at home, enabling him to better thrive in both domains. He now takes off two evenings a week, never works Sundays, and has had his first nonworking holiday, much to the delight of his family. He now describes his two non-work evenings as his "recovery sessions."

Reclaiming family time is good for you, for your family, and for your employer. But in addition, it is an opportunity to reframe the strongly held belief that the more hours we work, the more successful we are. The joy and fulfillment that result from having the time to fully attend to your family are sources of energy that never end.

14

Five Questions New Working Parents Should Ask Themselves

by Jackie Coleman and John Coleman

Quick Takes

- What does each parent actually want?
- What are the financial needs and constraints?
- What roles will each person play?
- Who's losing when?
- How can we stay close to each other?

The demands of both work and parenting are rising. Those employed in full-time work are often working more, but they are also parenting more. Researchers at UC Irvine found that parents in 11 countries spend nearly twice as much time with their kids as they did 50 years ago, with moms spending almost an hour more each day than in 1965 and dads spending nearly an hour each day with kids (as compared with 15 minutes in 1965).[1] Pew has found that dads now see parenting as just as central to their identities as moms do (though moms still parent more), and households with kids are now 66% dual income, versus 49% in 1970.[2] It is no surprise, given these time commitments, that 50%–60% of parents find work-life balance difficult.

When we decided to start a family years ago, our lives were very different. We slept in. We had more free time. We had different jobs and different working hours. Our financial situation was simpler. Our decision to become parents has been worth every trade-off, but it changed nearly everything in our working and personal lives. We've seen other couples experience the same shifts, through Jackie's prior work as a marriage counselor and John's experience as an executive. And based on that personal and professional experience, we encourage working couples who are new to parenting or are considering becoming parents to start the conversation by asking five questions. These questions are great to ask up front but are worth revisiting over time or when you have additional kids to make sure each person in the relationship is being heard and that your family stays on a firm foundation.

What does each parent actually want?

Men and women now often have more freedom to choose work inside or outside the home. As previously noted, an increasing number of women work outside the home, and according to recent surveys, a small but growing number of men are choosing to raise children full-time.[3] But cultural norms still place immense pressure on a couple. When we had our first child, Jackie originally planned to return to work following a short maternity leave, but ultimately she decided to take an extended period of time to stay home with our children. This was a perfectly valid choice and the one she ultimately wanted to make—but nonetheless she felt enormous pressure to return to work. Conversely, many women would love to pursue their careers but feel pressure to stay at home with children. And men still are often assumed to be better suited to working outside the home, rather than to staying home to raise a family.

Depending on your social circles, there can be overwhelming pressure to prioritize either work or family—navigating an ambitious career or creating flexibility to spend more time with kids. There is no right answer to this question, but there is a right answer for you and your family. And the answer starts with honesty and openness with yourself and each other. What do each of you really want? Ask the question frequently, as the answer may change over time.

What are the financial needs and constraints?

Few of us are free from financial constraints. They are the reality within which we operate. When working parents have kids, a sober evaluation of finances—how much money you want, how much you need, and how much you have—is a foundation for interpreting the constraints under which each family operates. Some people do not have a choice to navigate two-career households, because of childcare needs or health issues, for example, while some must choose the dual-career path due to financial demands. In the United States, each child costs approximately $230,000 to raise—$12,350 to $14,000 per year—and according to Care.com, day care costs more than $10,000 per year, on average, while the average cost of a nanny is more than $28,000 per year.[4] The costs of rearing children are real and meaningful. Each family's financial situation is different, but a clear-eyed evaluation of that situation is critical in order for working parents to properly evaluate the choices they make.

What roles will each person play?

Before having kids (or early on), it is helpful to be clear about who will be responsible for what, while noting that you'll likely also need to be flexible and step in for one another when necessary. Simple division of labor can make day-to-day decisions less stressful. Who pays the bills? Who takes out the trash or does the dishes? Who is responsible for dropping off or picking up the kids from school? Who will stay home from work if the child is sick? Research has shown that frankly working out the division of household labor (particularly if that division is fair) can help eliminate the tendency of "partners to express displeasure toward one another as they completed their chores," and while couples always need to be open to flexibility and helping one another, outlining a mutually understood view of household roles can be extraordinarily helpful in minimizing conflict.[5]

Who's losing when?

Jobs sometimes require moves. Financial needs sometimes require jobs that are not fun. Be honest about who is losing in decisions that require tough choices, and make sure it's not the same person every time.

Relationships require compromise. Decision by decision, one person may have to be prioritized over the other, but over a happy life together, one person cannot lose or win every time. For example, we have witnessed one partner in a relationship receiving a great job offer that requires a move, which may be fine, but when it happens again and again, the partner forced to adapt each time can quickly feel taken advantage of. If one partner feels that they always have to make the trade-offs, they should speak up. And each partner in the relationship must be open to listening to the concerns of the other.

How can we stay close to each other?

While juggling work and kids, it can be easy to neglect your spouse or partner. And if the relationship is failing or festering, both work and kids become infinitely more difficult. It is important to keep your relationship and each individual's mental, physical, and spiritual health prioritized over all else—including over kids and jobs. What will prioritizing your relationship look like, realistically, in the chaos of work and kids? How often will you go on dates? Can you carve out time for meaningful conversation each day? This may mean allotting money for a babysitter for one night per week, spending a day away from work to reconnect with your partner, or finding time to share a long lunch together. Perhaps the most important thing to "solve for" in the complex work-and-family dynamic is one another, and discussing in advance the rules of the road for sustaining your relationship can be essential as the burdens of work and parenting pile up.

Parenting can be remarkably rewarding. The decision to become a parent is not for everyone. But for partners considering the balance of work and parenting—as we have experienced time and time again, both in a marriage counselor capacity and in our personal experience—openly discussing the ways to make that complex dynamic work will lead to happier and healthier relationships and careers. If you and your partner are considering having children or are thinking through your current balance of work and parenting, we encourage you to ask these five questions of each other before you embark on the journey.

Adapted from "5 Questions New Working Parents Should Ask Themselves," on hbr.org, May 16, 2018 (product #H04BM6).

Win at Work by Leaning In at Home

by Stewart D. Friedman

Quick Takes

- Seek out four-way wins—small changes that can benefit work, home, community, and yourself

- Diagnose what's not working and what you wish you could do to fix it

- Talk to those around you about what matters most

- Try a small change for a brief period of time

Research shows that many men want to have richer lives, with greater emotional engagement and joy in their family lives and bigger contributions to their households.[1] But they face substantial barriers at work, in their homes, and inside their own heads.

Just as women need support from their organizations and their families to surmount the hurdles of fear and tradition, men need help in getting past the roadblocks that keep them from engaging more fully as caregivers and homemakers. And, of course, for women to advance in the world of work, men must advance in the world of home. The really good—seemingly paradoxical—news is that when men find smart, creative ways to lean in at home, they also perform better at work.

Getting Past What Holds Men Back

Traditional gender stereotypes are prisons for men, too, and hold many back from trying. Men may wonder: What if I'm just not a good dad? What if my friends perceive me as unmanly because I'm doing "women's work"?

What if my children see me as a poor role model because I'm not the main breadwinner? What if my boss thinks I'm less committed because I'm not at the office as much as the other guys at my level?

How does a man garner the courage to act, despite these worries, and get his boss and coworkers to encourage him to have breakfast with his family, leave work in time to pick up kids at school, and be truly focused on his family when he's with them instead of constantly checking his digital device about work matters?

Even in unsupportive work environments, men can make high-yield adjustments to make things better at work, at home, in the community, and for themselves (mind, body, spirit)—pursuing what I call "four-way wins." These are often small changes, designed to benefit key stakeholders in all parts of their lives. And that's what makes them work.

Diagnose, Dialogue, and Discover

For over a decade, students in my classes, as well as thousands of employees in hundreds of companies, have found that three steps make it possible for men to overcome the obstacles and lean in more at home in ways that benefit their careers at the same time.

Step 1—Diagnose

Figure out what's not working for you and what you wish you could do to ameliorate the situation. What's the problem? Your spouse isn't happy with your involvement? You're missing your children's childhoods? Your commute is too long? You're exhausted? You're distracted by work at home and by home while at work?

Asking these kinds of questions often produces these knee-jerk reactions:

- There is no solution that will work because my boss would never approve changes.

- I can't ask for something that's just for me and my family because it's selfish.

- I know I'm not happy but I don't see how things can improve, short of leaving my job.

To get to the next step, it helps to find a peer coach (or two)—someone preferably outside your immediate work circle—to brainstorm potential fixes. I have never seen anyone voice a problem for which someone else, with a fresh perspective, could not find solutions worth trying, especially if these solutions have real prospects of benefiting others.

Step 2—Dialogue

Talk to those around you—at work and at home—who matter most to you about what they really expect of you, how you're doing, and what you could do better. More often than not, what we think others expect of us is greater than (or a bit different from) what they actually expect of us. For example, you might think that your wife wants you home for dinner, when in fact it's the morning routine—getting the kids up and off to school—that is actually important to her as she is also trying to get to work early. Or you might think that your coworkers see being at work until very late as a sign of your commitment and great performance, when they actually view it as an indication of your inefficiency, as in, why can't you get your work done faster so that you don't need to be here this late?

Find out exactly what your important stakeholders need from you. Once you know more about what they actually expect, then you're ready for the next step.

Step 3—Discover

Try a small change for a brief time—a week or a month—and keep front of mind the benefits not to you (you will not forget those, I promise) but to key people at work (increased productivity because you'll be less distracted by family issues, have more energy, and be more committed to the organization), to people in your family, and to your friends and community.

Experiments and Their Impact

My research team studied what hundreds of people did when each was asked to design and implement an experiment for a four-way win. We observed many kinds of experiments; these were most popular:

- **Rejuvenating and restoring.** Take care of your mind, body, or spirit. Example: Start an exercise regimen program and watch carefully for the ripple effects at home, at work, and in the community as your energy increases and social connections strengthen.

- **Focusing and concentrating.** Be present for one person or task at a time. Example: Unplug from all digital media for one evening per week to connect with your family and friends to engage more fully and with less distraction at work.

- **Time-shifting and replacing.** Work remotely or during different times to increase efficiency and improve productivity. Example: Stay at work later on Tuesday and get in earlier on Thursday, or work on Saturday instead of Monday.

- **Delegating and developing.** Reallocate tasks to free up time, increase trust, and develop others' skills. Example: Give work to junior people on your team who are eager to learn and prove themselves, while freeing up your time for more important activities.

- **Exploring and venturing.** Take small steps toward doing something new that better aligns what you do with what you aspire to do. Example: You and your wife would like to have regular family dinners at home, but neither of you knows how to cook. Take a cooking class together and learn a new skill, strengthen your relationship, save money by buying groceries instead of getting takeout, and eat healthier because you're consuming fewer processed foods.

An experiment is limited by time and has measurable outcomes. While you believe that your request will not diminish or interfere with the work you produce—and indeed will enhance your productivity because you'll be happier, healthier, more energized, less distracted, more committed to the team, or more relaxed (or all of the above)—the proof will be in the results, and your colleagues and family will be the judges. Because you're experimenting, make it clear that after the agreed-on duration, if the experiment is not working for them, then you will return to the status quo or try something else.

No one has anything to lose, and all have something to gain. More often than not, when approached with this goal—to make it a win for all concerned—people around you might surprise you with their reasonableness.

When you invest intelligently in being a better father and see how this makes you more confident in your parenting skills and happier in your marital relationship, you become less distracted at work, are more energetic, and have a clearer focus on business results that matter. You begin to gain more confidence, which helps you overcome your anxieties about what others might think as you do more at home or spend less time at the office. Here are some examples of men who've done so.

Peter wanted to leave work earlier than usual to get home to his newborn son:

> *After my son was born, I found myself excited to get home to see him. These early departures have forced me to be much more disciplined with my time and helped prompt me to delegate work to my very capable and enthusiastic colleagues. I more than exceeded my original goal of leaving early one or two times per week and surprisingly found myself less overwhelmed at work than I was previously. My idea for the next phase of this experiment is to coordinate departure times among my peers, such that one of us covers the "after-hours" time slot each day of the week.*

Leonard, a financial services professional, wanted to spend more one-on-one time with family members. He and his wife committed to and carried through on a date night, and he played tennis with his 6-year-old son. But the biggest gain was in building his relationship with his 2-year-old daughter, who had previously been "a Mommy's girl." "I feel more productive, motivated, and focused as a result of this experiment. Since my home life is better, I can now allow myself to concentrate more on work when necessary without guilt that my home life is suffering."

Joseph, a research team leader at a pharmaceutical company, conducted an experiment to become more systematic about how he used his time at work and saw dramatic improvements at work, at home, and in his community. He made more family dinners, read to his children nightly, and missed no parent-teacher conferences, and his family reported that he now "always delivers." His research team was happier and more productive as a result of both his increased delegation and his "managing up to minimize 'reactive' work."

The results can be dramatic, but usually the interventions are fairly simple. One man tried creating a shared calendar with his wife—a no-brainer, right? It resulted in him missing fewer family commitments and being able to better set expectations of workload and plan the production schedule with his team at work. And he gained a new admiration for his wife's ability to manage the children's complex schedule while working full-time herself. This in turn led to a better marital relationship. Another told me that he started doing the dishes regularly and taking on more chores around the house. Not only did this give him more time at home doing things with his children, but it dramatically improved his relationship with his in-laws and his wife, removing what had been a source of stress in his life that had affected both his home and his work.

What we have seen over and over again is that no matter what the experiment—whether it's about disconnecting from 7:00 to 10:00 p.m. for one evening a week, coming in late two mornings to go to the gym, leaving early a day a week to coach, scheduling group meetings between 10:00 and 3:00 so members can leave early or come in late and not miss important group meetings, or any number of minor adjustments—productivity usually increases at work because employees are happier and more focused on results that matter, while retention increases because they are more committed.

Employers, this is not charity. This is not capitulation. And—though it has gotten a lot of attention as such—this is certainly not a women's issue. Helping men to be more active at home, if that's what they want, makes good business sense. It's wise to encourage employees to engage in dialogues with important people in their lives and to experiment with small changes that can enrich their families, enhance their engagement with their

community, and improve their health—all while en-
hancing your bottom line. By making it easier for men
to live fuller lives, employers are indirectly contributing
to paving the way for the women in their lives to give
more of themselves to their work and careers. And children—the unseen stakeholders at work—win, too. We as
a society are all the beneficiaries.

*Adapted from "Men: Win at Work by Leaning In at Home," on hbr.org, April 22,
2013 (product #H00AIC).*

Working Dads Need "Me Time," Too

by Alyssa F. Westring and Stewart D. Friedman

Quick Takes

- Beware of dropping everything that isn't work or family
- Create experiments to fold self-care into your schedule
- Focus on rejuvenating and restoring activities
- Accept that you may struggle at first

Dads are now increasingly engaged in childcare and household responsibilities, in addition to demanding jobs. They report levels of work-family conflict on par with (and, in some cases, higher than) mothers.[1] In addition, fathers who give higher-than-average levels of childcare, ask for paternity leave, or interrupt their careers for family reasons are harassed more at work, receive worse performance evaluations, and get paid less than men who either don't have kids or don't spend much time with them. And when fathers ask for flextime, they're often even more penalized than mothers are for making the same request.[2]

We need to recognize that working fathers, like working mothers, are susceptible to the "putting everyone else first" challenge of modern working-parenthood. We're already seeing this start to happen, and this increased visibility will hopefully lead to the systemic interventions we know work best. But in the meantime, how can individual dads start solving the problem of work-life conflict?

We set out to study working fathers of young children in our Total Leadership program—a widely recognized leadership development program that focuses on integrating four areas of life (work, home, community, and self) for improved performance in all four. The process starts with each participant diagnosing what matters most to him and engaging in dialogues with key stakeholders (spouse, boss, kids, and so on). Each participant then experiments with new ways of getting things done that serve all the different parts of their lives; they pursue "four-way wins."

We conducted an in-depth analysis of 36 working fathers of young children (under age three) who participated in this program as part of their Wharton Executive MBA. At the beginning of the program, it was clear that these fathers were skipping sleep, exercise, healthy eating, spiritual growth, and relaxation for the sake of their work and family responsibilities. Indeed, at the start of the experiment, they rated their satisfaction with their personal well-being as an average of 4.3 on a scale from 1 (not at all satisfied) to 10 (fully satisfied). This is in contrast to their reported satisfaction with work and with family, which were both rated significantly higher, with averages of 7.4 and 6.5, respectively. In other words, they were putting everyone else first—and themselves last.

So it wasn't surprising that when asked to design experiments to enhance performance in all areas of their lives, the most popular type of experiment for these new dads was "rejuvenating and restoring" (as compared to, say, planning or time-shifting). R&Rs involve taking care of yourself (for example, changes in diet or physical activity, doing meditation, taking vacation, etc.) to increase capacity and performance at work, in your family, and in the community via positive spillover—indirect effects that ripple out from the self to other parts of life. In an earlier study of the nine kinds of experiments, 57% of program participants completed an R&R. However, 75% of those in our working fathers sample did so, indicating a greater need for this sort of change in their lives.[3]

After their conversations with key stakeholders and some intensive coaching, the fathers in our sample implemented their experiments over the course of the subsequent 12 to 15 weeks. One decided to do yoga for three hours each week, with the expectation that it would "improve my physical fitness, mental concentration at work and school, outward confidence, and show importance of exercise to my kids and other stakeholders." Another committed to "exercise three times regularly a week because this will allow me to have more energy at home for the limited time I have for my wife and kids, providing me with the energy at work to handle stress better, be more patient, and be a much better leader . . . it will allow me to regain the health and peace of mind I so desperately need for myself."

The goal is not for participants to implement their experiments perfectly, exactly as designed. Instead, the purpose is to gain experience with trying new ways of doing things and thereby increase one's confidence and competence in one's capacity to initiate change that's truly sustainable. We were not surprised to find that many participants struggled to implement their well-being initiatives exactly as designed, given the intensive demands of their work, school, and family responsibilities.

Yet, even for those who struggled to fully follow through on attending anew to their personal needs as they had mapped out in the designs for their experiments, there was much growth and an increase in optimism. For instance, one father wrote that "this experiment and the introspection I have gained has taught me that without a healthy 'you' it is very difficult to excel or be your very best in other areas." Another wrote, "Giving time to oneself is very important. In our daily lives which have become so wired and busy, we hardly do that. Exercise and diet is just one of the ways to achieve that." Just as with working moms, several of the dads noted the importance of caring for oneself as a foundation for caring for others. One father aptly wrote, that "I heard someone refer to this as the analogy of putting on the oxygen mask before helping others, and that is how I feel."

At the conclusion of our program, we asked participants to again rate their satisfaction with the different areas of their lives. Working fathers' satisfaction with the "self" domain improved from 4.3 to an average of 6.5, a statistically significant increase. And these gains in the personal domain were not accomplished at the cost of reduced satisfaction in other domains. Significant increases were also observed, as satisfaction with work and

FIGURE 16-1

Taking care of yourself doesn't mean letting others down

Working dads who consciously took more time for themselves for 12–15 weeks felt better about their personal well-being—and their work and families.

	Satisfied with personal well-being	Satisfied with work	Satisfied with family
Before taking time for self	4.3	7.4	6.5
After taking time for self	6.5	8.4	8.5

Scale: 1 = Not at all satisfied; 10 = Fully satisfied

family also rose, to an average of 8.4 and 8.5, respectively (see figure 16-1). On separate measures, participants also reported significant improvements in physical health and mental health, as well as a reduction in stress.

All of us fall into the trap of saying we can't afford to take time for ourselves; what's important about our study is that it shows that on the contrary, we *have* to take time for ourselves in order to effectively serve others. It isn't only moms who tend to put themselves at the bottom of the list, nor is it only mothers who can benefit from more self-care. Today's fathers need it, too.

Adapted from content posted on hbr.org, June 13, 2014 (product #H00UY3).

Bringing Your Dad Network Together

by Scott Behson

Quick Takes

- Create a fatherhood network to provide you with relationships, advice, and support

- Start with other dads you know from work and your kids' schools

- Stop worrying about feeling awkward or coming off as too eager

- Make spending time with your dad network a regular part of your schedule

You're at an industry conference. You've been chatting with a new acquaintance after the keynote address. You've hit it off and have some things in common. He works in the same industry you do and faces a lot of the same challenges at his work. Do you exchange information, stay in touch, and follow up with him to talk shop and give each other help and advice? Because you understand the importance of networking, you probably do.

You're at your kid's soccer game. You've been chatting with a new acquaintance on the sideline. You've hit it off and have some things in common. He lives in the same town and your kids are of similar ages, and he faces a lot of the same challenges juggling work demands with being a good dad. Do you exchange information, stay in touch, then follow up with him to exchange ideas and give each other help and advice? Despite the fact that you understand the importance of networking, you probably don't.

This example represents a missed opportunity, an unforced error that working dads make all the time. The networking skills you bring to your career can help you build a fatherhood network. And a fatherhood network accomplishes in our home lives the same positive outcomes as professional networking does for our careers: mutually beneficial relationships, advice, information, and encouragement.

Networking is critically important for working fathers. So many of us lack an extensive friendship and peer support network, at a time in our lives when we need these the most. But our longtime friends move away, get married, have kids, and become just as busy as we are juggling careers and fatherhood. Further, most men over 30 find it hard to make new friends—it often feels awkward and vulnerable to make that first step.[1] Finally, many of us feel guilty about our long hours, so much so that we devote our nonwork time to our kids and to giving our spouses some well-deserved free time.

Our lack of fatherhood networks makes it hard for us to attend to our needs for well-being, friendship, and mutual support—things that make us more effective, happier fathers in the long run. As this dad articulates:[2]

> *I don't need friendships now any less than I did when I was younger, and I certainly feel their absence in my life today, sometimes very acutely. But the realities of being an adult and a dad with a career seem to preclude making new emotionally sustaining friendships. So it begs the question: Where do dads get friends?*

That's where your networking skills come in. It's time to stop worrying about feeling awkward or coming off as too eager. There's ample opportunity to build fatherhood networks both at work and at home, if we just put in some effort up front.

Good networkers leverage workplace connections

If we don't already have good work friends who face similar work-life challenges, we should try to cultivate these relationships. Simple actions like asking coworkers about their kids can start the process. We can build on this by organizing weekly lunch groups or after-work happy hours. Then take it a step further—set up a time for your group to meet outside of work—this is especially easy if your kids are at playground age.

In addition to informal networking, many employers host employee resource groups (ERGs) around employee interests and identities. You can join a parenting ERG to meet fellow working parents, share ideas, and learn from those who have older kids. If your firm doesn't yet have a group for dads, you might want to start one. You'll likely get lots of interest and support—after all, Deloitte has hosted a successful dads' group since 2010.[3]

Good networkers seek out new opportunities

Our children almost certainly go to school and participate in sports and other activities. These are greatly
underutilized places to connect with fellow dads.
Schools and day cares often host events and volunteer
opportunities for parents. The PTA is often only 75%
women, and many men volunteer and attend school
functions held at night. Most schools would be happy to
host a "Dad's Group" if a dad or two decided to start one.

Good networkers not only make chitchat with other
dads at kids' activities, they take the next step. After all,
these people have similar interests and challenges, are
clearly also interested in being involved dads, and can
provide mutual emotional and instrumental support.
Next time, step out of your comfort zone, exchange
emails and phone numbers, and then organize a guys'
night. As this dad says:

> I think fatherhood is the ultimate bonding oppor-
> tunity for men, at least for those who are fortunate
> enough to experience it. I don't know whether to
> call it a club or a fraternity or whatever, but there's
> something bonding about fatherhood.

Good networkers make networking a regular part of their schedules

The next step is to arrange for regular get-togethers. Regularity matters—trust and friendship are built over time around shared experiences. I am lucky that my neighbor started a Wednesday night tradition of inviting his local guy friends, most of whom are balancing interesting and rewarding careers with the rigors of being fathers to young kids, to hang out by the fire pit in his backyard. Because this is a standing group on a regular night, we are more likely to schedule the time and be able to attend, and because it's a large group, it's OK if, some weeks, life gets in the way of attending. We've come to call this brilliant innovation "Beer Fire."

I have greatly benefited from Beer Fire—it's relaxing and fun, and I always learn a little something from everyone I talk to. Our conversations naturally gravitate to what we all share in common—our careers, our kids, and how we try to juggle it all. We've discussed a wide range of topics including kids' chores and allowances, the merits of local swimming and dance programs, and even how to negotiate with our bosses for more flexible schedules.

Good networkers create their own opportunities

Following my neighbor's example, I organized Thursday night "Zoom happy hours" with several of my college friends during the spring 2020 height of social distancing. Of course, we talk about old times, but more often we discuss how we are dealing with work from home and online school. Just as the pandemic changed remote work, it is changing dad networks, too—keeping in touch with old friends actually seems easier.

Whatever you are interested in, there's probably a group of peers eager for the opportunity to join you and buddy up. With a little thought, planning, and putting yourself out there, you could organize a hiking group, or a Saturday morning pickup basketball game, gather to watch *Monday Night Football*, form a cover band to jam together, or join a local volunteering organization.

Good networkers leverage existing organizations

Many community organizations and churches have started parenting groups, and many are even developing groups specifically for dads. One dad's experience demonstrates how important these can be:

My church was my entry point for meeting so many fellow dads. Now I'm involved with the Knights of Columbus one or two nights a week. We do a lot of good, which is very fulfilling, but it also gets me out of the apartment and keeps me from feeling isolated.

Also, now I know so many good dads—some my own age, others older, others younger, and we can share advice and learn from each other. I've been helped so much by their advice and example in being a better dad and husband.

On a broader scale, City Dads Group was founded in New York City in 2008 by two new dads who were frustrated by the lack of resources, groups, and other supports for fathers.[4] At first, they simply got together with some fellow dads to meet at playgrounds and parks. Word spread, so they started an online "meetup" group page, which then grew into dozens of dads getting together. There are now City Dads Groups in 40 metro areas around the country—hosting dad-and-kid events, dads-only social events, and even new-dad boot camps in which expecting dads learn from experienced dads. This may be a good place to start your fatherhood network.

Good networkers make things happen

However you decide to get started, applying your career networking skills and making the effort to develop and maintain a network of dads is well worth it. Fatherhood networks give us access to advice, encouragement, and most importantly, the friendships that can make all the difference as we juggle our careers with our most important life role—being great fathers.

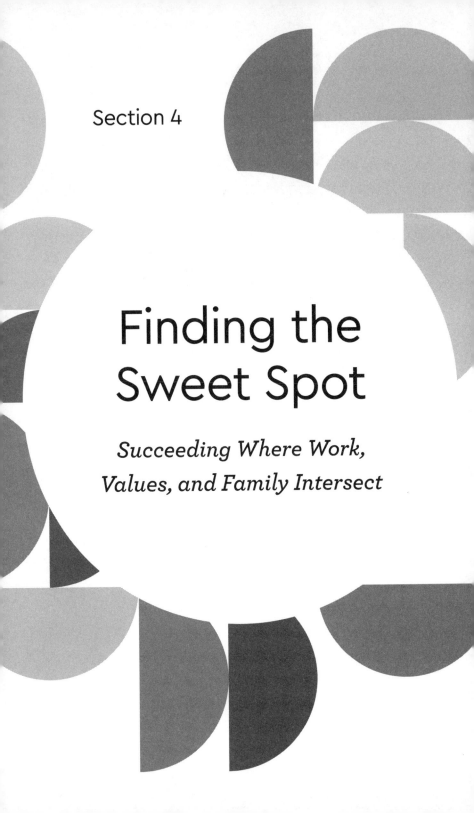

Section 4

Finding the
Sweet Spot

*Succeeding Where Work,
Values, and Family Intersect*

How Our Careers Affect Our Children

by Stewart D. Friedman

Quick Takes

- The quality of time parents spend with children matters more than quantity

- Excessive psychological involvement with work has a detrimental effect on children's well-being

- Overall *time* parents spend working does not influence children's mental health

- Experiment with creative ways to be available, physically and psychologically, to your children

What working parent hasn't felt guilty about missing soccer games and piano recitals? When there are last-minute schedule changes at work or required travel to a client site, it's normal to worry that you're somehow permanently scarring your little one.

But how *does* our work affect our children's lives? About two decades ago, in a study that surveyed approximately 900 business professionals ranging from 25 to 63 years old, across an array of industries, Drexel University's Jeff Greenhaus and I explored the relationship between work and family life and described how these two aspects of life are both allies and enemies.[1] In light of the deservedly increased attention we're now paying to mental health problems in our society, it's worth taking a fresh look at some of our findings on how the emotional lives of children—the unseen stakeholders at work—are affected by their parents' careers. Our findings help explain what's been observed since our original research about how children are negatively affected by their parents being digitally distracted, also known as "technoference," and by the harmful effects of stress at work on family life.

Most of the research on the impact of parental employment on children looks at whether or not mothers work (but not, until very recently, fathers); whether parents work full- or part-time; the amount of time parents spend at work; and the timing of parental employment in the span of children's lives.[2] Our research went beyond matters of time, however, and looked, in addition, at the inner experience of work: parental values about the importance of career and family, the psychological interference of work on family life (that is, we are thinking about work when we are physically present at home with our family), the extent of emotional involvement in a career, and discretion and control about the conditions of work.

All these aspects of parents' careers, we found, correlate with the degree to which children display behavior problems, which are key indicators of their mental health. We measured them with the Child Behavior Checklist, a standard in the child development research literature that has not been used in other research in organizational psychology. Unfortunately, to date, the specific effects of parents' work experiences (not time spent at work) on children's mental health have still not been a priority for research in this field. They should be, for this is yet another means by which work can have important health consequences. Here are some of the highlights of what we observed.

For *both* mothers and fathers, we found that children's emotional health was higher when parents believed that family should come first, regardless of the amount of time they spent working. We also found children were better off when parents cared about work as a source of challenge, creativity, and enjoyment, again, without regard to the time spent. And, not surprisingly, we saw that children were better off when parents were able to be physically available to them.

Children were more likely to show behavioral problems if their fathers were overly involved psychologically in their careers, whether or not they worked long hours. And a father's cognitive interference of work on family and relaxation time—that is, a father's psychological availability, or presence, which is noticeably absent when he is on his digital device—was also linked with children having emotional and behavioral problems. On the other hand, to the extent that a father was performing well in and feeling satisfied with his job, his children were likely to demonstrate relatively few behavior problems, again, independent of how long he was working.

For mothers, on the other hand, having authority and discretion at work was associated with mentally healthier children. That is, we found that children benefit if their mothers have control over what happens to them when they are working. Further, mothers spending time on themselves—on relaxation and self-care—and not so much on housework, was associated with positive outcomes for children. It's not just a matter of mothers being at home versus at work, it's what they do when they're at home with their nonwork time. If mothers were not with their children so they could take care of themselves, there was no ill effect on their children. But to the extent that mothers were engaged in housework, children were more likely to be beset by behavior problems.

Traditional roles for fathers and mothers are surely changing since we conducted this research. But it's still the case that women carry more of the psychological burden of parental responsibilities. Our research showed that taking time to care for themselves instead of for the additional labor of housework strengthens mothers' capacities to care for their children. And fathers are better able to provide healthy experiences for their children when they are psychologically present with them and when their sense of competence and their well-being are enhanced by their work.

The good news in this research is that these features of a parent's working life are, at least to some degree, under their control and can be changed. We were surprised to see in our study that parents' *time* spent working and on childcare—variables often much harder to do anything about, in light of economic and industry conditions— did not influence children's mental health. So, if we care about how our careers are affecting our children's mental health, we can and should focus on the value we place on our careers and experiment with creative ways to be available, physically and psychologically, to our children, though not necessarily in more hours with them. Quality time is real.

Adapted from content posted on hbr.org, November 14, 2018 (product #H04NLJ).

19

Four Ways to Teach Your Kids About Work

by Sabina Nawaz

Quick Takes

- Practice time management with your children
- Teach leadership ideas through reading
- Explore values by discussing real-life dilemmas
- Help your children learn to frame problems in multiple ways

As a leader, you probably juggle many things at work and at home. You're not alone. Most executives I coach struggle with balancing parenting and work duties. They worry that they aren't spending enough time with their children, and they'd like to help their children learn from their experience and avoid mistakes they've made.

What if you could maximize your time by making progress on work challenges while spending time with your children and helping them learn important skills in the process? Given my own challenges with balancing multiple priorities, I've learned a few ways to make the most of my time with both work and family, and I've shared these tips with my clients, many of whom have adopted similar practices. And the tips don't take any additional time. You can increase time with your children without losing work time or adding more to your already full plate. By doing things a bit differently, you benefit your task list, your children, and yourself.

Here are four ways you can spend time with your kids while getting work done and teaching them important lessons along the way.

Practice time management together

One of your primary jobs as an executive is to anticipate the future and set a course to achieve success. This often takes concentrated time, away from the demands of back-to-back meetings. Many executives I coach take two hours a week to create white space. But unless you plan well in advance, it's hard to find two hours of contiguous time each week.

Starting when he was eight years old, my older son would sit down with me once a quarter and help me block out white-space time for the next quarter. We would also block out time for vacations, shows, and volunteering. Because we carve out this time together, it helps me maintain a stronger boundary for family time. By helping me, my son appreciates the variety of my job responsibilities, not just what he sees from videos of my keynote talks. He's also learned how to plan ahead to create balance and dedicate time to think strategically, and he's picked up some other time management tricks. As a result, he creates time blocks on his calendar to ensure he has enough time for large projects that can't be done in one sitting. It has reduced the amount of last-minute drama in our household.

Teach leadership ideas through reading

Harry Truman once said, "Not all readers are leaders, but all leaders are readers." I'm much better at reading lots of books than at remembering lots of information from those books. Therefore, as I read each book, I tag passages that I'd like to go back to later. My sons compile all the tagged sections into one document. They curate my notes because I pay them, but you can also involve your kids by creating a game or competition such as answering trivia questions from the books at the dinner table. After all, these aren't books they'd willingly pick up. Not only does this save me time and help me retain what I've read, but it also teaches my children at an early age about leadership topics from expert authors. Yesterday our dinner table conversation included the benefits of having mirror neurons and showing empathy when we want to improve our influence skills. It was a direct outcome of the book one of my sons is currently working on.

Explore values through discussing real-life dilemmas

Last month I struggled with a situation at work in which, if I acted according to my values, I would risk losing a large percentage of my revenue. It would be easy to pretend with my children that everything was business as usual. However, it wasn't easy on my sleep. As I struggled with what to do, my husband and I discussed the dilemma (while protecting confidential information) with our boys. We laid out the situation, which values it was violating, and the potential risks of upholding my values. It was a difficult choice, but I decided to act in favor of my values.

I'd forgotten about the event until my older son said to me the other day, "Mom, I want to have integrity in how I talk to my science fair partner." Curious, I asked, "What does integrity mean to you?" and was surprised to hear him remind me, "Mom, you always say integrity is doing the right thing when nobody is looking." Having an open discussion about a work struggle benefited my son in a way I hadn't anticipated.

Help children learn to frame problems in multiple ways

A common way that my coaching clients struggle is when they make assumptions about their adversary's motivations during an interpersonal conflict and choose destructive actions based on that one conclusion. For example, Raymond, a tech executive, was recently convinced that his peer Jay wanted to discredit him and take over his team. Raymond jumped to this conclusion because Jay had interrupted during his presentation about his new project in front of the CEO. Rather than assume the worst of Jay, I told Raymond that he should lean into his natural tendency for storytelling and create not one but three separate stories about what Jay's motivations could be. Raymond's alternative stories were that perhaps Jay was very excited by Raymond's idea and wanted to add his own ideas to it, or that Jay was less aware of interpersonal interactions and was someone who tended to interrupt others as well. This allowed Raymond to confront his assumptions and examine other possibilities.

You can share this tactic with your children as a game my family calls Multiple Meanings. We take turns creating stories from observations of people and events on trips to and from school. For example, if we see a man with tattooed arms and a sleeveless vest walking rapidly on the sidewalk, we might make up a story that he's late for work because his car broke down, so he's walking fast to get help. Maybe he owns a tattoo parlor across the bridge and is a walking advertisement for his business. Or maybe he's meeting someone in the park and is running late. Our children then use the skill when they're upset about something at home or at school. This is especially helpful when my sons argue and come to me for mediation. To reduce the heat in the conflict, I ask: "What other meanings can you make about why your brother borrowed your Lego airplane?" The goal is to be able to calm themselves down and be more empathetic, so they approach someone else with curiosity instead of judgment.

We spend a lot of our waking hours working. We also invest a lot in educating our children on academic subjects, physical activities, and the arts. But we treat these two activities separately. By involving our children in our work activities, we can teach our children key skills from our own experience, while maintaining quality time both at work and at home.

Adapted from "4 Ways to Teach Your Kids About Work (Without Adding More to Your Plate)," on hbr.org, April 18, 2018 (product #H04AG9).

20

How to Spend Your Parenting Time and Energy Wisely

by Amy Jen Su

Quick Takes

To make the best of your finite time and energy as a parent, align your contribution and your passion.

- Determine what you do that your children value the most

- Reflect on which parenting activities motivate and inspire you the most

- Prioritize tasks and experiences that fulfill both of these

- Delegate or spend less time on activities that don't fulfill either

C arole came into our coaching meeting looking especially frustrated. As an IT leader at her
company, she was under constant time pressure,
and her week had gotten off to a stressful start. "I move
mountains to wrap up work early on Tuesdays to get to
my teen daughter's soccer practice, only to feel like she
doesn't even care I'm there! I don't know what to do.
Sometimes, if I don't go, I feel guilty. When I do make
the time, I feel underappreciated. It's a no-win situation."
This mounting frustration, she shared, had left her distracted and less engaged over the following two days,
both at home and at work.

I hear scenarios like this frequently from clients who
are working parents. And I have faced them myself. Both
at work and as parents, we place high expectations on
ourselves to be effective, successful, and to make the best
use of our limited time. Misusing that time, in either
realm, can feel like a double failure.

Despite the exhaustion of the early years, things are
simpler the younger our children are. Newborns' needs
can be summed up in a short list beginning with food,
care, and love—and we do it all. As they start school

and advance through their teen years, our ability to find our highest and best use as parents becomes more complex. As we juggle work and home, with our time always squeezed, how can we ensure that we are spending our parenting time and energy in the right ways, especially as our children age and change? It begins with two questions.

Define Your Contributions and Passions as a Parent

Instead of ending up feeling underappreciated or guilty about the time you do or don't spend with your kids, you can proactively triage your parenting time and energy. I recommended that Carole try an approach I use with leaders at work: prioritizing according to contribution and passion. To do this, think of one of your children and answer the following questions:

1. **Contribution:** Which of the activities I do, tasks I perform, or types of support I provide does my child value the most right now? (Answer for each child you have individually.)

2. **Passion:** Which activities, tasks, or types of support give me the most motivation, inspiration, or energy as a parent?

TABLE 20-1

Parenting time 2×2

		Contribution	
		Low	High
Passion	**High**	*Q3: Low/High* Deemphasize activities that may be outdated and are no longer as relevant or of high value to your child.	*Q1: High/High* Prioritize activities where contribution to your child and your passion match.
	Low	*Q4: Low/Low* Eliminate or delegate to the extent possible.	*Q2: High/Low* Manage the energy impact. Ask for help or delegate where possible.

Determine Parenting Time and Stay Relevant Using a 2×2

You can take the two criteria above and create a corresponding 2×2 set of quadrants to help guide decisions around parenting time (see table 20-1).

Quadrant 1: High contribution/High passion

This is the sweet spot of parenting time, as these activities add value for your child and give you an energy boost. As Carole looked at her answers to the questions, she realized her best times with her daughter included activities where she both contributed and from which she derived passion, including their mutual interest in technology, going for runs together, or researching things her daughter was interested in. These are the activities where parents and children truly bond. She agreed to start prioritizing her parenting time for things that fell in quadrant 1.

Quadrant 2: High contribution/low passion

Activities in quadrant 2 can be tricky as our kids will have needs that may drain our energy. The answer isn't to stop doing them but to minimize their energy impact or identify resources that can provide help. For example, Carole realized that she was tired after filling out school forms, but that this was something that her husband didn't mind doing. They compared their contributions and passions and looked for places where her quadrant 2 matched his quadrant 1 and vice versa. Working parents who have a caregiver can optimize their resources further.

Quadrant 3: Low contribution/high passion

Our kids' interests and needs are always changing. Quadrant 3 is a real danger zone for parents because often we find ourselves engaging with our kids around activities or interests we love but our kids don't actually value.

Even worse, we risk putting inadvertent pressure on our children to engage in an activity because they know we care about it as the parent.

Therefore, it is critical to set up regular checkpoints with our kids to understand how they regard our contributions as they age. As a working parent myself, I use a ritual each year where I sit down with my son at the start of each school year and ask him the top three things I do as a mom that he values the most. When he was younger, I made a list of all the things we did together and had him put a star next to his favorite three items. Now that he is older, it's a much more open-ended conversation. Then, to find the sweet spot, I line up his top three contributions against my top three passions.

It's been amazing for me to see how this sweet spot of time for us has evolved through the years. When he was younger, even when we had a nanny, he most valued and I most enjoyed doing a certain number of drop-offs or pickups from school during the week, attending a karate practice, and tucking him in at bedtime. As a teen now, he doesn't value and in fact doesn't want me to be seen at school drop-off or pickup! Instead, he values my time at key volleyball tournaments on the weekends, especially the ones out of town.

By staying in tune with who he is now, versus being grounded in the past, I am better able to ensure staying in quadrant 1 versus quadrant 3.

Quadrant 4: Low contribution/low passion

When things are busy or when you try to do everything, you can end up engaged on autopilot in activities that neither add value nor bring you passion. It is easy for parents to fall into habits and assumptions and continue doing what they have always done without reconsideration. This can lead to frustrating moments like the one Carole experienced at her daughter's soccer practice. She was used to going to her daughter's practice on Tuesdays, even though it turned out that this didn't bring value or energy for either of them anymore.

If you find yourself in quadrant 4, it's best to stop doing those activities that are no longer relevant for you or your child and gain back precious time.

Operationalize into Your Calendar

Learning the quadrants is only the first step. If you don't have a plan for putting your insights into action, your good intentions to spend time with your kids in the best ways will get swept up in your long list of to-dos. Use your calendar to carve out and protect time for quadrant 1 activities.

Use pre-blocks

Pre-block your calendar with major school events like performances or teacher conferences as soon as that information is available. It's not perfect, and there will be plenty of weeks where work travel or deliverables get in the way, but proactively planning will enable you to have an honest discussion ahead of time when you can't be there.

Color-code

Color-coding your calendar can help you take a longer view of how you spend your time. Carole highlighted any quadrant 1 time she spent with her daughter in orange. It helped her to see the trend line over a longer arc of time versus expecting herself to be perfectly balanced in any given week. Color-coding is not intended to make you feel guilty (as working parents often do), but rather to serve as a cue to adapt as needed.

Stay in Active Dialogue

Even with the best of triaging or planning time with your kids, it is important to stay in active conversation with them to keep them involved and adapt to changes.

Use look-aheads

Throughout the year, bring your family together to see what is upcoming on the calendar. For families with older children, you can designate a day and time such as Sunday morning at breakfast to have everyone pull up laptops and calendars, and scan for the upcoming week. Especially with multiple kids, where sibling rivalry over parents' time and attention can exist, the family look-ahead can help to ensure that parenting time is distributed fairly.

For younger children, use visuals such as wall calendars or large whiteboards with pictures denoting when you have work or other obligations. Often, the uncertainty and inconsistency of when you will or won't be home are what kids struggle with the most.

Talk about it

Talking to our kids regularly about where and how we spend our time gives us a chance to model good communication and time management practices. If the amount of time you are (or aren't) spending with children is a road bump in your family's progress, have a conversation rather than avoiding it or letting things fester. Ask your kids to be active problem solvers with you in finding more satisfying ways to spend time together. Let them see you ask for help from other family members, neighbors, or your spouse when you get into a time bind.

Ultimately, Carole felt much more in control and effective as she became intentional around her parenting time decisions. Carole and her daughter collaboratively agreed that Carole should stop leaving work early for soccer practices. Instead, her daughter encouraged her to use that time she was at practice to focus on work and then come to pick her up afterward. Her daughter shared that, as a teen, what she valued now was the car time after practice, when they could talk and catch up one-on-one on each other's day with few distractions.

• • •

My hope for myself and all working parents like Carole is that the practices outlined in this article will help us find new confidence in the ways we spend our time and alleviate guilt about letting go of some things we simply don't have enough time to do. These changes can increase our fulfillment at work and help maintain meaningful relationships with our kids as they grow up.

How Working Parents Can Regain Control over Their Lives

by Stewart D. Friedman and Alyssa F. Westring

Quick Takes

- Embrace values-driven leadership as a working parent
- Think about what matters most to you, and why
- Come up with five values and write them down
- Communicate those values to the people who matter to you most

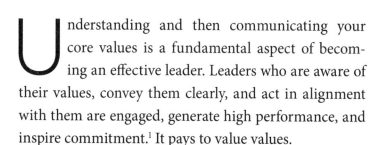

U nderstanding and then communicating your core values is a fundamental aspect of becoming an effective leader. Leaders who are aware of their values, convey them clearly, and act in alignment with them are engaged, generate high performance, and inspire commitment.[1] It pays to value values.

Working parents, who face a significant leadership challenge in raising children, can benefit from value-driven leadership. Often overwhelmed by the struggle to make smart decisions about when, where, and how to invest our attention, not many of us working parents stop and reflect on our values. Instead, we tend to internalize the values of our society and people around us, usually unconsciously. Social media amplify the impact of social comparisons, making it harder to stay centered, to know ourselves. When we lack a clear set of values, or fail to communicate them, we're rudderless and have no guiding compass.

When we identify and express our values, we can more readily use what we truly care about as the basis for making decisions, large and small. In our research, we've found that people who bring a well-articulated set of core values to all parts of life experience less stress, greater harmony, and better performance at home, in their communities, and for themselves personally.

To spur your thinking as you consider your own values—those you aspire to embody in your career, as a parent, and in the rest of your life—here are a few examples listed by working parents in our research on the application of leadership principles to the art of parenting:

Achievement. A sense of accomplishment or mastery, striving to be the best.

Adventure. New and challenging opportunities, excitement, risk.

Collaboration. Close, cooperative working relationships, being part of a team.

Courage. A willingness to stand up for your beliefs and do the difficult thing—despite any fears.

Generosity. Being known by others as one who gives.

Humor. The ability to laugh at yourself and at life.

Love. That indescribable feeling when your kids run up to give you a hug after work.

Responsibility. Doing what you say you will do.

Spirituality. Believing there is something greater than human beings.

As you contemplate, remember that values are relatively stable over time and rather broad, not tied to specific people, places, and times.[2] They are usually influenced by significant events in your life history.

If you've never done so, start by thinking about what matters most to you and why. Try to come up with about five values and write them down. Don't limit yourself to the examples we listed. If you're stuck, do an online search for a list of values and pick those that most accurately represent you, and then think about why, with reference to the road you've traveled so far. Of course, you can always revise, so allow yourself to be as candid as possible.

The next step is communicating those values to the people who matter most to you. Start with your partner(s) in parenting—those with whom you're raising children together. This could be a spouse, but it could also be an ex-spouse, a close relative, a life partner, or a dear friend. It's useful to ask them to do this exercise on their own and to then talk over your distinctive and your common values. Just as leaders in groups and organizations need to establish shared values, parenting partners, too, must identify the values that inform their lives.

Take Emma and Marcos Lopez, from Houston, Texas, who participated in our Parents Who Lead workshop. Emma is a management consultant and Marcos, a former captain in the army, is an investment manager. They have a 4-year-old and a 7-year-old. They both listed "career success" as a core value.

But this confused them because they sensed that they held quite different attitudes about their work. Looking more deeply, it turned out that career success meant something different to each of them. Emma remembered a period during her adolescence when her family struggled to make ends meet after her father was laid off. She realized that the intense stress her family experienced then played a significant role in forming who she became. That's why, for Emma, career success primarily means having sufficient funds stashed away and enough transferable job skills so she does not have to worry about economic security.

For Marcos, a veteran who embraced the clear hierarchy in the military ranking system, career success meant achieving promotions and seniority. Certainly Marcos, like Emma, cares about economic security, but he does not equate it with success. Similarly, Emma cares about recognition, but it is not paramount when she thinks of what success means.

Articulating these distinctions helped them better understand the way they each approach their careers. And when it came to thinking about what they wanted for their future, they were able to envision how they could support each other more carefully and compassionately, not only in their respective careers but also in their roles as mother and father to their kids.

Most people assume their partners know each other's values. Yet even people who enjoy close long-term relationships are often surprised when they reveal their core values to each other. Indeed, research has shown that we're not nearly as accurate as we think when it comes to judging the values, experiences, and goals of those closest to us.[3] You might be surprised by what you find when you share your deepest-held values.

For Emma and Marcos Lopez, discussing their values shed new light on one another, despite the fact that they've known each other for 12 years. Marcos would often get frustrated by Emma's always-on, 24/7 availability for her consulting work. He'd frequently find her lit by the glow of her laptop in bed after he assumed that she was turning in for the night. It was only after learning more about this aspect of Emma's family history and the traces it left that both he and Emma came to understand that her work ethic was driven, at least in part, by worries about losing her economic security and a fear that she wouldn't get placed on future consulting projects if she didn't perform at a high level on the current one.

For Emma and Marcos, clarifying and communicating their values was an essential first step in becoming values-driven leaders in all parts of their lives. From there, they were able to create a vision for the future that incorporated both of their definitions of career success and other shared and unique values they identified. They were able to strengthen their bonds with the people who matter most to them by communicating these values, and to experiment with a few innovations in how they enact their values in their daily lives.

Mining the ore from the mountain of your experience to identify and then describe your core values to your partners in parenting, and being genuinely curious about what they mean, is a crucial part of becoming a parent who leads. Your values are the basis for making mindful choices in both the everyday and the momentous decisions we face. And the foundation on which your children stand is strengthened when you take to heart the leadership challenge of striving to act in a way that's in accord with what you care about most.

Adapted from "How Working Parents Can Regain Control Over Their Lives," on hbr.org, March 5, 2020 (product #H05GJ6).

\

Epilogue

Take Things One Day at a Time

Lessons in Entrepreneurship from a Gay Father of Triplets

by Dan Pallotta

Quick Takes

- You never know what the future will hold
- You don't need to force your will on every situation
- Don't let negative feelings interfere with your commitment
- Lean on your partners

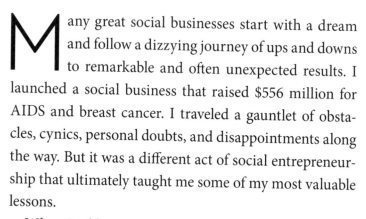

M any great social businesses start with a dream and follow a dizzying journey of ups and downs to remarkable and often unexpected results. I launched a social business that raised $556 million for AIDS and breast cancer. I traveled a gauntlet of obstacles, cynics, personal doubts, and disappointments along the way. But it was a different act of social entrepreneurship that ultimately taught me some of my most valuable lessons.

When I told my parents in my junior year at Harvard that I was gay, they sent me to see Dr. Goldblatt—my cardiologist. What else would you expect first-generation, Italian, blue-collar folks to do but send their kid to the best Jewish doctor in town? I saw him, he told me I'd be fine, and we shared a hysterical laugh together. And I was fine. But my parents were saddened by the thought that I'd never have children, and I was too. If you were gay in 1980, you didn't think having kids was a possibility.

Twenty-five years later, things had changed. My partner and I were exploring how we might have children. We tried international adoption. Big disappointment. None of the countries that the agencies worked with would allow gay parents to adopt. Next we tried adopting through the County of Los Angeles. More disappointment: Its first priority is to reunite kids with birth parents, even after placement. We didn't want that kind of heartbreak. Then we tried private open adoption. But after conversations with about 15 different birth mothers over two long years, we had gotten nowhere. If my partner and I hadn't had one another to lean on through all these letdowns, there's no way we could have kept going.

After all this, we decided to try to have our own biological children. This was a road fraught with even more uncertainty and potential despair. Again disappointment. Because of a medical issue with our egg donor, our first attempt at a pregnancy failed. "Find another egg donor," the doctor told us. It was not what we wanted to hear. We wanted *that* embryo to turn into a pregnancy. Today, I'm glad that it didn't, as you'll see. We found another egg donor, but then a medical issue surfaced with our surrogate. "Find another surrogate," our doctor told us. At this point, we didn't have a lot of hope left in us. Four years into the journey, it felt like this was just not meant to be.

But we forged ahead, despite the dwindling odds. We had 10 frozen embryos. Seven died in the thawing process. The three that remained were not of great quality. The doctor recommended transferring all three and gave us a 35% chance of a pregnancy.

Then, finally, things turned around.

Ten days later, our new surrogate was pregnant. Six weeks later, her first ultrasound revealed not one heartbeat, but three. She carried the kids to 34.5 weeks—the average triplet pregnancy goes about 32 weeks. Our three beautiful children were born on October 16, 2007: two girls and a boy, and my partner and I each got to have our own biological children.

In my wildest dreams back in 1980, I could never have predicted any of this. And all of it taught me a few things that apply to any endeavor of entrepreneurship:

- You never know what the future is going to bring. So stop predicting your own failure. Your job is to take the next indicated step in front of you. Shorten your horizon. One day at a time. Don't think beyond these eight hours, unless you have to for logistical purposes. On your worst days, get through it one hour at a time.

- Don't force your will on every situation. Don't think that you have to drive every pitch and every product to success. It could well be that the investor who says no was going to be your worst nightmare. And it could be that the obstacle that kept you from launching the product you were obsessed with gave rise to a better idea and transformed your business. A larger intelligence than your own may be at work: Let it do some of the heavy lifting. Its imagination may be infinitely more creative than your own. Steve Jobs didn't invent the iPod. Someone brought it to him.

- Don't let your feelings interfere with your commitment. You may not "feel" like going out and making another pitch. You may feel too depressed to draft the next iteration of the business plan. But what difference do your feelings make? Do what you have to do regardless of how you feel about it.

- Lean on your partners. Don't be afraid to tell them when you're having a bad day, or when you feel like giving up, or feel like a loser, or are in a state of total despair. Feelings are temporary. They're unstable. They pass. And they pass much more quickly when they're shared.

And last but not least, when you're having a personal crisis, a cardiologist isn't the worst person you could see.

Adapted from content posted on hbr.org, January 28, 2010.

NOTES

Chapter 1

1. Brad Harrington, "Maximizing the Employee Experience: How Changing Workforce Dynamics Are Impacting Today's Workplace," Boston College Center for Work & Family, 2018, https://www.bc.edu/content/bc-web/schools/carroll-school/sites/center-for-work-family/research/work-life-flexibility.html.

2. Brad Harrington, "Behind the Data on Breadwinner Mothers," *New York Times,* June 3, 2013, https://www.nytimes.com/roomfordebate/2013/06/03/what-are-fathers-for/behind-the-data-on-breadwinner-mothers.

Chapter 2

1. Pew Research Center, "Breadwinner Moms," *Social & Demographic Trends*, May 29, 2013, https://www.pewsocialtrends.org/2013/05/29/breadwinner-moms/5/; Pew Research Center, "Modern Parenthood," *Social & Demographic Trends*, March 14, 2013, https://www.pewsocialtrends.org/2013/03/14/modern-parenthood-roles-of-moms-and-dads-converge-as-they-balance-work-and-family/; Brad Harrington, Fred Van Deusen, and Jennifer Sabatini Fraone, "The New Dad: A Work (and Life) in Progress," Boston College Center for Work & Family, 2013, https://www.bc.edu/content/dam/files/centers/cwf/research/publications3/researchreports/The%20New%20Dad%202013_A%20Work%20and%20Life%20in%20Progress.

2. Scott Behson, *The Working Dad's Survival Guide: How to Succeed at Work and at Home* (Melbourne, FL: Motivational Press, 2015).

Chapter 3

1. "2019 Employee Benefits," SHRM, n.d., https://www.shrm.org/hr-today/trends-and-forecasting/research-and-surveys/pages/benefits19.aspx.

2. "Paternity Leave," DOL Policy Brief, U.S. Department of Labor, n.d., https://www.dol.gov/sites/dolgov/files/OASP/legacy/files/PaternityBrief.pdf.

3. "Expanded Paid Parental Leave," Boston College Center for Work & Family, n.d., https://www.bc.edu/content/dam/files/centers/cwf/research/publications/researchreports/Expanded%20Paid%20Parental%20Leave-%20Study%20Findings%20FINAL%2010-31-19.pdf.

4. Emily Paisner, "Back-to-School 2020: Care.com Survey Reveals What's Really on the Minds of Working Parents," *Care@Work blog*, August 6, 2020, https://workplace.care.com/workingparentssurvey.

5. McKinsey & Co. and LeanIn.Org, *Women in the Workplace 2020*, n.d., https://wiw-report.s3.amazonaws.com/Women_in_the_Workplace_2020.pdf.

6. "Labor Force Participation—Women," FRED Economic Data, November 6, 2020, https://fred.stlouisfed.org/series/LNS11300002.

7. Promundo and Dove Men + Care, "Helping Men Care," 2018, https://promundoglobal.org/wp-content/uploads/2018/06/Promundo-DMC-Helping-Men-Care-Report_FINAL.pdf.

Chapter 4

1. Melissa J. Williams and Larissa Z. Tiedens, "The Subtle Suspension of Backlash: A Meta-analysis of Penalties for Women's Implicit and Explicit Dominance Behavior," *Psychology Bulletin* 142, no. 2 (2016): 165–197, https://pubmed.ncbi.nlm.nih.gov/26689089/.

2. Ashleigh Shelby Rosette, Jennifer S. Mueller, and R. David Lebel, "Are Male Leaders for Seeking Help?," *Leadership Quarterly* 25, no. 5 (2015): 749–762, https://www.sciencedirect.com/science/article/pii/S1048984315000223.

3. Kerry Roberts Gibson, Dana Harari, and Jennifer Carson Marr, "When Sharing Hurts," *Organizational Behavior and Human Decision Processes* 144 (2018): 25–43, https://www.sciencedirect.com/science/article/abs/pii/S0749597815302521.

4. Timothy A. Judge, Beth A. Livingston, and Charlice Hurst, "Do Nice Guys—and Gals—Really Finish Last?," *Journal of Personality and Social Psychology* 102, no. 2 (2012): 390–407, https://psycnet.apa.org/record/2011-27429-001.

5. L. A. Rudman and P. Glick, "Feminized Management and Backlash Toward Agentic Women," *Journal of Personality and Social Psychology* 77, no. 5 (1999): 1004–1010, https://pubmed.ncbi.nlm.nih.gov/10573877/.

6. Janine Bosak et al., "Be an Advocate for Others, Unless You Are a Man," *Psychology of Men & Masculinity* 19, no. 1 (2018): 156–165, https://psycnet.apa.org/buy/2016-59613-001.

7. William A. Gentry et al., "How Displaying Empathic Concern May Differentially Predict Career Derailment Potential for Women and Men Leaders in Australia," *Leadership Quarterly* 26, no. 4 (2015): 641–653, https://www.sciencedirect.com/science/article/pii/S1048984315000600.

8. Victoria L. Brescoll and Eric Luis Uhlmann, "Can an Angry Woman Get Ahead?," *Psychological Science* 19, no. 3 (2008): 268–275, https://pubmed.ncbi.nlm.nih.gov/18315800/.

9. Agneta H. Fischer, Alice H. Eagly, and Suzanne Oosterwijk, "The Meaning of Tears," *European Journal of Social Psychology* 43, no. 6 (2013): 505–515, https://onlinelibrary.wiley.com/doi/abs/10.1002/ejsp.1974.

10. Daphna Motro and Aleksander P. J. Ellis, "Boys Don't Cry: Gender and Reactions to Negative Performance Feedback," *Journal of Applied Psychology* 102, no. 2 (2017): 227–235, https://pubmed.ncbi.nlm.nih.gov/27808525/.

11. Corinne A. Moss-Racusin et al., "When Men Break Gender Rules," *Psychology of Men & Masculinity* 11, no. 2 (2010): 140–151, https://psycnet.apa.org/buy/2010-07392-008.

12. Laurie A. Rudman, "Self-Promotion as a Risk Factor for Women," *Journal of Personality and Social Psychology* 74, no. 3 (1998): 629–645, https://psycnet.apa.org/record/1998-00299-006.

13. Bradley P. Owens, Angela S. Wallace, and David A. Waldman, "Leader Narcissism and Follower Outcomes," *Journal of Applied Psychology* 100, no. 4 (2015): 1203–1213, https://pubmed.ncbi.nlm.nih.gov/25621592/.

14. Kathryn J. Holland et al., "Sexual Harassment Against Men," *Psychology of Men & Masculinity* 17, no. 1 (2016): 17–29, https://psycnet.apa.org/buy/2015-17472-001.

15. Jennifer L. Berdahl, "Harassment Based on Sex," *Academy of Management Review* 32, no. 2 (2007): 641–658, https://www.jstor.org/stable/20159319?seq=1#page_scan_tab_contents.

16. Laurie A. Rudman and Kris Mescher, "Penalizing Men Who Request a Family Leave," *Journal of Social Issues* 69, no. 2 (2013): 322–340, https://spssi.onlinelibrary.wiley.com/doi/abs/10.1111/josi.12017.

17. Tessa L. Dover, Brenda Major, and Cheryl R. Kaiser, "Diversity Policies Rarely Make Companies Fairer, and They Feel Threatening to White Men," hbr.org, January 4, 2016, https://hbr.org/2016/01/diversity-policies-dont-help-women-or-minorities-and-they-make-white-men-feel-threatened.

18. Ben Barry, "What Happens When Men Don't Conform to Masculine Clothing Norms at Work?," hbr.org, August 31, 2017, https://hbr.org/2017/08/what-happens-when-men-dont-conform-to-masculine-clothing-norms-at-work.

Chapter 5

1. Haley Swensen, "Engaged Dads and the Opportunities for and Barriers to Parenting in the United States," New America, June 17, 2020, https://www.newamerica.org/better-life-lab/reports/engaged-dads-and-opportunities-and-barriers-equal-parenting-united-states/.

2. Gretchen Livingston and Kim Parker, "8 Facts About American Dads," FactTank, Pew Research Center, June 12, 2014, https://www.pewresearch.org/fact-tank/2019/06/12/fathers-day-facts/.

3. McKinsey & Co. and LeanIn.Org, *Women in the Workplace*, 2020, n.d., https://wiw-report.s3.amazonaws.com/Women_in_the_Workplace_2020.pdf.

4. Scott Schieman, Leah Ruppanner, and Melissa A. Milkie, "Who Helps with Homework?," *Journal of Family and Economic Issues* 39 (2018): 49–65, https://link.springer.com/article/10.1007/s10834-017-9545-4.

5. Allison Damiger, "The Cognitive Dimension of Household Labor," *American Sociological Review* 84 no. 54 (2019), https://journals.sagepub.com/doi/abs/10.1177/0003122419859007.

6. "So You Want to Be a Male Ally for Gender Equality?," Promundo, n.d., https://promundoglobal.org/resources/male-allyship/.

7. "CPE Checklist," Fair Play, n.d., https://www.fairplaylife.com/the-cards/cpe.

8. Scott Coltrane, "Research on Household Labor," *Journal of Marriage and Family* 62, no. 4 (2000): 1208–1233, https://onlinelibrary.wiley.com/doi/abs/10.1111/j.1741-3737.2000.01208.x.

9. David G. Smith and Mady Wechsler Segal, "On the Fast Track: Dual Military Couples Navigating Institutional Structures," in *Visions of the 21st Century Family: Transforming*

Structures and Identities, vol. 7 (Bingley, UK: Emerald Publishing, 2013), https://www.emerald.com/insight/content/doi/10.1108/S1530-3535(2013)0000007011/full/html?utm_source=Trend MD&utm_medium=cpc&utm_campaign=Contemporary _Perspectives_in_Family_Research_TrendMD_1.

10. Scott Coltrane et al., "Fathers and the Flexibility Stigma," *Journal of Social Issues* 69, no. 2 (2013): 279–302, https://spssi.onlinelibrary.wiley.com/doi/abs/10.1111/josi.12015.

Chapter 6

1. The quotes and the prioritization exercise are adapted from my book, S. Behson, *The Working Dad's Survival Guide: How to Succeed at Work and at Home* (Melbourne, FL: Motivational Press, 2015), https://www.amazon.com/Working-Dads-Survival -Guide-Succeed/dp/1628651946/ref=sr_1_3?crid=16TZZ89OCY KXC&dchild=1&keywords=working+dads+survival+guide&qid =1603680940&s=books&sprefix=working+dads%2Cstripbooks %2C152&sr=1-3.

2. James M. Citrin, *The Career Playbook: Essential Advice for Today's Aspiring Young Professional* (New York: Crown, 2015), https://www.thecareerplaybook.com/.

3. Amy Saltzman, *Downshifting: Reinventing Success on a Slower Track* (New York: Harper, 1992).

4. My forthcoming book, *The Whole Person Workplace* (Highlands Ranch, CO: Authors Place Press, 2021) explores this topic in more detail.

Chapter 7

1. Bureau of Labor Statistics, "Employment Characteristics of Families—2019," news release, April 21, 2020, https://www.bls.gov/news.release/pdf/famee.pdf.

2. Liana S. Leach et al., "Prevalence and Course of Anxiety Disorders (and Symptom Levels) in Men Across the Perinatal Period,"

Journal of Affective Disorders 190 (2016): 675–686, https://pubmed
.ncbi.nlm.nih.gov/26590515/#affiliation-1.

3. Cleber José Aló de Moraes and Tania Mara Marques Granato,
"Becoming a Father: An Integrative Review of the Literature on
Transition to Fatherhood," *Psicologia em Estudo* 21, no. 4 (2017):
557–567, https://www.researchgate.net/publication/315762206
_BECOMING_A_FATHER_AN_INTEGRATIVE_REVIEW_OF
_THE_LITERATURE_ON_TRANSITION_TO_FATHERHOOD.

4. Bianca Wordley, "The Men Who Find the Transition to Fatherhood Most Difficult," *Essential Baby*, March 16, 2018, http://www
.essentialbaby.com.au/pregnancy/news-views/the-men-who-find
-the-transition-to-fatherhood-most-difficult-20180315-h0xjs2.

5. Aló de Moraes and Marques Granato, "Becoming a Father."

6. Samantha J. Teague and Adrian B. R. Shatte, "Exploring the
Transition to Fatherhood," *JMIR Pediatrics and Parenting* 1, no. 2
(2018), https://www.ncbi.nlm.nih.gov/pmc/articles/PMC6715057/.

7. Brad Harrington and Jamie Ladge, "The New Dad: Exploring
Fatherhood Within a Career Context," Boston College, June 2010,
https://www.researchgate.net/publication/259266390_The_New
_Dad_Exploring_Fatherhood_within_a_Career_Context
_Boston_College.

8. Harrington and Ladge, "The New Dad."

Chapter 9

1. Hugh Wilson, "The Millennial Dad at Work," DaddiLife, May 18,
2019, https://www.daddilife.com/the-millennial-dad-at-work/.

2. Marianna Hunt, "The Best Companies to Work for as a New
Father—with the Most Paid Paternity Leave," *Telegraph*, February
22, 2020, https://www.telegraph.co.uk/money/consumer-affairs/
best-companies-work-new-father-paid-paternity-leave/.

3. Ian Dinwiddy, "The Part Time Lawyer," DaddiLife, November 8,
2019, https://www.daddilife.com/tom-the-part-time-lawyer/.

4. "Why Dad to Dad Mentoring Matters at Work," DaddiLife, November 25, 2019, https://www.daddilife.com/why-dad-to-dad-mentoring-matters-at-work/.

Chapter 10

1. "When Everyone Can Work from Home, What's the Office for?," PWC Remote Work Survey, June 25, 2020, https://www.pwc.com/us/en/library/covid-19/us-remote-work-survey.html.

Chapter 11

1. Gretchen Livingston and Kim Parker, "Growing Number of Dads Home with the Kids," Pew Research Center, June 12, 2016, https://www.pewresearch.org/fact-tank/2019/06/12/fathers-day-facts/.

2. Stefanie K. Johnson and David R. Hekman, "Women and Minorities Are Penalized for Promoting Diversity," hbr.org, March 23, 2016, https://hbr.org/2016/03/women-and-minorities-are-penalized-for-promoting-diversity.

Chapter 12

1. Brad Harrington, Jennifer Sabatini Fraone, Jegoo Lee, and Lisa Levey, "The New Millennial Dad: Understanding the Paradox of Today's Fathers," The New Dad Research Series, Boston College Center for Work & Family, 2016, https://www.bc.edu/bc-web/schools/carroll-school/sites/center-for-work-family/research/work-life-flexibility1.html.

Chapter 14

1. Preeti Varathan, "Modern Parents Spend More Time with Their Kids Than Their Parents Spent with Them," Quartz, November 30, 2017, https://qz.com/1143092/study-modern-parents-spend-more-time-with-their-kids-than-their-parents-spent-with-them/.

2. Gretchen Livingston and Kim Parker, "8 Facts About American Dads," FactTank, Pew Research Center, June 12, 2019, https://www.pewresearch.org/fact-tank/2019/06/12/fathers-day-facts/.

3. Gretchen Livingston, "Growing Number of Dads Home with Kids," Pew Research Center, June 5, 2014, https://www.pewso cialtrends.org/2014/06/05/growing-number-of-dads-home-with -the-kids/.

4. Kathryn Vasel, "It Costs $233,610 to Raise a Child," CNN Money, January 9, 2017, https://money.cnn.com/2017/01/09/pf/ cost-of-raising-a-child-2015/index.html; Care.com editorial staff, "Child Care Costs More in 2020, and the Pandemic Has Parents Scrambling for Solutions," Care.com, June 15, 2020, https://www .care.com/c/stories/2423/how-much-does-child-care-cost/.

5. Wendy Klein, Carolina Izquierdo, and Thomas N. Bradbury, "The Difference Between a Happy Marriage and a Miserable One: Chores," *Atlantic*, March 1, 2013, https://www.theatlantic.com/ sexes/archive/2013/03/the-difference-between-a-happy-marriage -and-miserable-one-chores/273615/.

Chapter 15

1. Stewart D. Friedman, "New Research on Working Parenthood," hbr.org, October 4, 2012, https://hbr.org/2012/10/new-research-on -working-parent; "Expanded Paid Parental Leave," The New Dad Research Series, Boston College Center for Work & Family, 2019, https://www.bc.edu/bc-web/schools/carroll-school/sites/center -for-work-family/research/work-life-flexibility1.html.

Chapter 16

1. Kristen M. Shockley, Winny Shen, Michael M. DeNunzio, Maryana L. Arvan, and Eric A. Knudsen, "Disentangling the Relationship Between Gender and Work–Family Conflict: An Integration of Theoretical Perspectives Using Meta-analytic Methods," *Journal of Applied Psychology* 102, no. 12 (2017): 1601–1635.

2. Sarah Thébaud and David S. Pedulla, "Masculinity and the Stalled Revolution: How Gender Ideologies and Norms Shape Young Men's Responses to Work–Family Policies," *Gender & Society* 30, no. 4 (2016): 590–617; Scott Behson, "What's a Working Dad to Do?" hbr.org, August 21, 2013, https://hbr.org/2013/08/whats-a-working-dad-to-do; Gayle Kaufman, "Barriers to Equality: Why British Fathers Do Not Use Parental Leave," *Community, Work & Family* 21, no. 3 (2018): 310–325.

3. Stewart D. Friedman and Alyssa Westring, "Empowering Individuals to Integrate Work and Life: Insights for Management Development," *Journal of Management Development* 34, no. 3 (April 2015): 299–315.

Chapter 17

1. Billy Baker, "The Biggest Threat Facing Middle-Age Men Isn't Smoking or Obesity. It's Loneliness," *Boston Globe*, March 9, 2017, https://www.bostonglobe.com/magazine/2017/03/09/the-biggest-threat-facing-middle-age-men-isn-smoking-obesity-loneliness/k6saC9FnnHQCUbf5mJ8okL/story.html.

2. The quotes and much of the advice in this article are adapted from my book: S. Behson, *The Working Dad's Survival Guide: How to Succeed at Work and at Home* (Melbourne, FL: Motivational Press, 2015).

3. Leah Eichler, "Double Duty: The Plight of the Working Dad," *Globe and Mail*, March 1, 2013, https://www.theglobeandmail.com/report-on-business/careers/career-advice/life-at-work/double-duty-the-plight-of-the-working-dad/article9213833/.

4. City Dads Group, https://citydadsgroup.com/.

Chapter 18

1. Stewart D. Friedman and Jeffrey H. Greenhaus, *Work and Family—Allies or Enemies?* (New York: Oxford University Press, 2000).

2. Rachel G. Lucas-Thompson, Wendy A. Goldberg, and JoAnn Prause, "Maternal Work Early in the Lives of Children and Its Distal Associations with Achievement and Behavior Problems: A Meta-analysis," *Psychological Bulletin* 136, no. 6 (2010): 915–942, https://www.apa.org/pubs/journals/releases/bul-136-6-915.pdf.

Chapter 21

1. Gang Wang et al., "Transformational Leadership and Performance Across Criteria and Levels," *Group & Organization Management* 36, no. 2 (2011), https://journals.sagepub.com/doi/abs/10.1177/1059601111401017.

2. Laura Parks-Leduc, Gilad Feldman, and Anat Bardi, "Personality Traits and Personal Values: A Meta-analysis," *Personality and Social Psychology Review* 19, no. 1 (2015), https://journals.sagepub.com/doi/full/10.1177/1088868314538548.

3. David A. Kenny and Linda K. Acitelli, "Accuracy and Bias in the Perception of the Partner in a Close Relationship," *Journal of Personality and Social Psychology* 80, no. 3 (2001): 439–448, https://psycnet.apa.org/record/2001-16719-006.

ABOUT THE CONTRIBUTORS

DAISY DOWLING, SERIES EDITOR, is the founder and CEO of Workparent, the executive coaching and training firm, and the author of *Workparent: The Complete Guide to Succeeding on the Job, Staying True to Yourself, and Raising Happy Kids* (Harvard Business Review Press, 2021). She is a full-time working parent to two young children. She can be reached at www.workparent.com.

TIM ALLEN, CEO of Care.com, oversees the company's strategic direction, leadership, and growth, all centered on one mission: to transform how families care for all they love. A 15-year veteran of media and technology company IAC, Tim has played pivotal roles shaping IAC brands like Vimeo and Ask.com, and he founded and ran IAC's Mosaic Group. A father to young twin boys, Tim relates to the challenges faced by working parents everywhere. He and his family reside in Austin, Texas.

SCOTT BEHSON is a professor of management and a Silberman Global Faculty Fellow at Fairleigh Dickinson University, and the author of *The Working Dad's Survival Guide* and *The Whole-Person Workplace*. He writes and consults on work-life policies and was a featured speaker at the White House and the United Nations. His most important roles are as husband and father, and he can be seen most often grading papers and writing articles in the car during his teen son's sports practices.

SUZANNE BROWN is a work-life balance speaker, consultant, and author of the award-winning books *Mompowerment: Insights from Successful Professional Part-Time Working Moms Who Balance Career and Family* and *The Mompowerment Guide to Work-Life Balance.* She helps companies become more balance-friendly and working moms create greater work-life balance. Find more practical tips to shift your mindset about balance and take action on www.mompowerment.com. In her downtime, you can find her on a nearby hiking trail or far-off adventure with her husband and their two young boys.

JACKIE COLEMAN is a former marriage counselor and most recently worked on education programs for the state of Georgia.

JOHN COLEMAN is a coauthor of the book *Passion & Purpose: Stories from the Best and Brightest Young Business Leaders.* Follow him on Twitter @johnwcoleman. Jackie and John have four sweet, mischievous kids ranging from newborn to seven years old. They keep life crazy, full, and fulfilling.

BRUCE FEILER is the author of seven *New York Times* bestsellers, including *Life Is in the Transitions*, *The Secrets of Happy Families*, and *The Council of Dads*, which inspired the hit NBC drama series. He's also the host of two prime-time series on PBS, and his two TED Talks on family and fatherhood have been viewed more than 2 million times. He lives in Brooklyn with his wife, Linda Rottenberg, and their identical twin daughters, Eden and Tybee. For more information, please visit brucefeiler. com.

STEWART D. FRIEDMAN, an organizational psychologist at the Wharton School, is author of three Harvard Business Review Press books—*Total Leadership: Be a Better Leader, Have a Richer Life*; *Leading the Life You Want: Skills for Integrating Work and Life*; and *Parents Who Lead: The Leadership Approach You Need to Parent with Purpose, Fuel Your Career, and Create a Richer Life*. He founded the Wharton Leadership Program, the Wharton Work/Life Integration Project, and Total Leadership, a management consulting and training company. His three grown children work in education. He hopes his two grandchildren will help us all heal our broken world.

BRAD HARRINGTON is the executive director of the Boston College Center for Work & Family and a research professor in the Carroll School of Management. Prior to his arrival at Boston College in 2000, Harrington was an executive with Hewlett-Packard Company for 20 years. He served in a wide range of global and business unit leadership roles in the United States and Europe. His research and teaching focus on career management and work-life integration, the changing role of fathers, and contemporary workforce management strategies. He is married to Dr. Annie Soisson, director of the Tufts University Center on Learning and Teaching, and is the father of three millennials.

ROGER JOHNSON is an associate professor of biology and biochemistry at Southern Virginia University, where he serves as the Division Chair of the Mathematics and Natural Sciences Division. During his time as a lead parent, he didn't persuade his children to become biologists, but he did teach his youngest how to become a chemist (i.e., cook).

W. BRAD JOHNSON is a professor of psychology in the Department of Leadership, Ethics, and Law at the United States Naval Academy and a faculty associate in the Graduate School of Education at Johns Hopkins University. He is the coauthor of *Good Guys: How Men Can Be Better Allies for Women in the Workplace*; *Athena Rising: How and Why Men Should Mentor Women*; *The Elements of Mentoring*; and other books on mentorship. Now that his three adult sons are out making the world more inclusive, he is busy coaching a new aspiring male ally, his 1-year-old grandson.

WHITNEY JOHNSON is the CEO of human capital consultancy WLJ Advisors, an Inc. 5000 2020 fastest-growing private company in America. One of the 50 leading business thinkers in the world (#14) as named by Thinkers50, Whitney and her team are expert at helping high-growth organizations develop high-growth individuals. She is the wife of one, and mother of two wonderful truth tellers (aka college-age children).

REBECCA KNIGHT is a freelance journalist in Boston whose work has been published in the *New York Times*, *USA Today*, and the *Financial Times*. She is the mom of two tweenage daughters.

HAN-SON LEE is the founder of DaddiLife, a platform and community for modern-day fatherhood, and a campaigner for change around dads at work. He is dad to one boisterous boy who's always keeping him on his toes.

DAVID M. MAYER is the John H. Mitchell Professor of Business Ethics in the Management and Organizations Area at the University of Michigan's Stephen M. Ross School of Business. His research sits at the intersection of leadership, ethics, and diversity. He is also the

proud father of Avery and Caleb and enjoys torment-
ing them with dad jokes. Follow him on Twitter @
DaveMMayer.

MARK MCCARTNEY is a leadership coach and a member of Oxford University's Saïd Business School coaching
community. He coaches working dads in leadership
positions wanting to thrive at work and home by imple-
menting a new set of recovery practices. He is dad to two
boys, 7 and 11, and husband to a wife who runs her own
business. Find more information at www.tofocus.co.uk.

SABINA NAWAZ is a global CEO coach, leadership keynote speaker, and writer working in over 26 countries.
She advises C-level executives in *Fortune* 500 corporations, government agencies, nonprofits, and academic
organizations. Sabina has spoken at hundreds of seminars, events, and conferences, including TEDx, and has
written for FastCompany.com, Inc.com, and Forbes.com.
She is lucky to have the support of her stay-at-home husband. She counts as successful any meeting that's free of
interruption by her two teenage sons or two dogs. A successful day is one spent with them. Follow her on Twitter
@sabinanawaz.

DAN PALLOTTA is an expert in nonprofit-sector innovation and a pioneering social entrepreneur. He is the
founder of Pallotta TeamWorks, which invented the

multiday AIDSRides and Breast Cancer 3-Days. He is the president of Advertising for Humanity and the author of *Charity Case: How the Nonprofit Community Can Stand Up for Itself and Really Change the World.*

EVE RODSKY is a lawyer and the founder of the Philanthropy Advisory Group, which advises high-net-worth families and charitable foundations on best practices for harmonious operations, governance, and disposition of funds. She is the author of *Fair Play: A Game-Changing Solution for When You Have Too Much to Do (and More Life to Live).* Eve and her husband Seth are raising their two sons and daughter to be gender justice advocates who pride themselves on knowing that taking out the garbage isn't complete until a fresh bag goes back in the bin.

DAVID G. SMITH is a professor of sociology in the College of Leadership and Ethics at the United States Naval War College. He is the coauthor, with W. Brad Johnson, of *Good Guys: How Men Can Be Better Allies for Women in the Workplace* and *Athena Rising: How and Why Men Should Mentor Women.* He is grateful for his two grown kids, who are an epidemiologist and video production director and continue to teach him important life lessons.

AMY JEN SU is a cofounder and managing partner of Paravis Partners, a premier executive coaching and leadership development firm. For the past two decades, she has coached CEOs, executives, and rising stars in organizations. She is the author of the Harvard Business Review Press book *The Leader You Want to Be* and coauthor of *Own the Room* with Muriel Maignan Wilkins. Amy is also a full-time working parent with a teenage son who is currently in high school.

JAMES SUDAKOW is the author of *Out of the Blur: A Delirious Dad's Search for the Holy Grail of Work-Life Balance* (2018), which tells his story of building and running a small business while raising a family.

HALEY SWENSON is an expert on work, gender, and inequality and the deputy director of the Better Life Lab, a work-life justice policy program based at the nonpartisan think tank New America. She is the author of the recent report "Engaged Dads and the Opportunities for and Barriers to Equal Parenting in the United States." Haley and her wife Alieza live and work in Utah, where they strive to be equal partners in caring for their large extended family and their two cats, Bertie and Shoshana.

ALYSSA F. WESTRING is the Vincent de Paul Associate Professor of Management and Entrepreneurship at DePaul University's Driehaus College of Business. She is the coauthor of *Parents Who Lead: The Leadership*

Approach You Need to Parent with Purpose, Fuel Your Career, and Create a Richer Life (Harvard Business Review Press, 2020). She is an award-winning educator and the director of research at Total Leadership. She has two school-age children and lives in Chicago.

HUGH WILSON is a writer for DaddiLife, and as an editor and journalist also writes across a wide variety of topics around modern-day family. He is father to two wonderful children whom he homeschools.

INDEX

coworkers (*continued*)
forming parenting alliances
with, 80–81
speaking with about your life
as a parent with, 81–82
cultural norms
pressures on parents and
parenting from, 121
See also masculine norms
culture. *See* organizational
culture

Dad Connect program,
DaddiLife website, 84
dad networks, 145–153
creating with allies and
coworkers at work, 83–84,
148
example of starting, 151
existing church and
community organizations
with, 151–152
importance of, for working
fathers, 147–148
networking skills for
starting, 146–147, 148,
153
scheduling on a regular
basis, 150
workplace connections
through, 148
See also support groups
dad transition. *See* fatherhood
transition
decision making

collaborating with partners
on, for gender equity, 43
time priorities in parenting
and, 173–177
using core values in, 182–183,
187
Deloitte, 148
Department of Labor, 23
DHG, 90
diagnose-dialogue-discover
approach, 129–132, 141
diversity training, 34–35
Dove Men + Care, 26
dual-income families. *See* two-
career families

egalitarian fathers
satisfaction at work of, 7
shared parenting good
intentions and reality for,
5–7
suggestions for catalyzing
change by, 10–12
emotional health of children,
and parents' work
experience, 158, 159–161
empathy, and masculine
norms, 31–32
Employee Benefits Survey,
Society for Human
Resource Management,
23
employee resource groups
(ERGs)
joining or starting, 10, 148

using as an example for
others, 19
four-way wins, from
experiments making small
changes, 129, 132–134, 141
Friedman, Stewart D., 127–137,
139–144, 157–162, 181–187
friendships, in dad networks,
147, 150, 153

gay parents, parenting lessons
learned by, 191–195
gender equity
acknowledging aspiration-
execution gap in, 41–42
aiming for equity versus
50-50 split in, 42
collaborating with partners
on decision making for, 43
Covid-19 pandemic's impact
on, 26
"double shift" of paid and
unpaid labor of working
mothers and, 39
halo effect of dad-friendly
companies for, 25–26
mental load of women's
"cognitive labor" for family
and, 39–41
percentage of daily tasks
done by fathers and, 39, 41
speaking up at work about
access to benefits and, 44
taking paternity leave and
benefits for, 23

gender policing, 35
gender roles. See also
masculine norms
barriers to work-family
balance and, 17–18
managers' lack of
understanding of, 9
men's involvement at home
and, 128–129
paternity leave and, 9
pressures to conform to
traditional concepts of,
16–17, 79
supporting partner's career
and, 43
goal setting, in parenting,
109–110
Greenhaus, Jeff, 158
groups. *See* dad networks;
employee resource
groups (ERGs); fathers'
groups at work; support
groups

Harrington, Brad, 3–14
Hastings College of the Law,
Flexibility Stigma Working
Group, 17
Herlihy, Virginia, 83
Hewlett, Sylvia Ann, 97
home life
diagnosing what's not
working in, 130
dialoguing about
expectations in, 131

Find fulfillment at home and at work with the HBR Working Parents Series

Advice for Working Dads

Advice for Working Moms

Communicate Better with Everyone

Getting It All Done

Managing Your Career

Taking Care of Yourself

FOR MORE, VISIT **HBR.ORG/BOOKS**

An all-in-one resource for every working parent.

If you enjoyed this book and want more guidance on working parenthood, turn to *Workparent: The Complete Guide to Succeeding on the Job, Staying True to Yourself, and Raising Happy Kids*. Written by Daisy Dowling, a top executive coach, talent expert, and working mom, *Workparent* provides all the advice and assurance you'll need to combine children and career in your own, authentic way.

AVAILABLE IN PAPERBACK
OR EBOOK FORMAT.